Real *Mysterious*
Pennsylvania

UFOs, Bigfoot, and
Other Weird Encounters
Casebook One

Really Mysterious Pennsylvania UFOs, Bigfoot and Other Weird Encounters Casebook One

By
Stan Gordon

Interested parties may contact Stan Gordon at:
P.O. Box 936, Greensburg, PA 15601

or via e-mail at paufo@comcast.net or phone: 724-838-7768.
Up-to-date information can be found at:
www.stangordon.info

ISBN 978-0-9666108-2-6

Library of Congress Control Number: 2010902305

First Edition

Printed in the United States of America

Edited by John David Kudrick

**Typesetting & Design by Michael Coe of Bulldog Design
www.bulldogdesign.us**

10   9   8   7   6   5   4   3   2

Contents

Dedication

This book of mysterious events is dedicated to my longtime friend and cohort, George E. Lutz. George and I began our investigative work together during the early 1970s, spending much time climbing hills, walking through and alongside streams, and searching the mountains and woods for evidence of strange creatures and UFO encounters. George is a retired Air Force officer and pilot, and is also an experienced outdoorsman. He has been a close friend of mine for many years, and we share memories of chasing after some very strange beasts that unfortunately we never had the opportunity to see.

Acknowledgements

I want to thank all of the volunteer members of the WCUFOSG, PCUFOR, PASU, and MUFON, and the many other researchers with whom I have had contact for their input on some of these cases. I also want to especially thank Charles Hanna and Robert McCurry for permission to use their artwork depicting some of these incidents.

My wife, Debbie, continues to stand behind my investigative efforts into these continuous odd happenings. It is with her love and support that I have been able to continue on my quest to find answers to these mysteries.

Introduction

The world is full of mysterious events, and at a very young age I was drawn to these mysterious subjects. Always interested in science and electronics, I spent much time outdoors collecting insects and other specimens to examine under my microscope. On more than one occasion, I probably came close to causing an explosion in my home with some concoction that I had created with my chemistry set.

Some of my favorite TV shows were The Outer Limits, Science Fiction Theater, One Step Beyond, and The Twilight Zone. But it was on my tenth birthday in 1959 that my life was suddenly drawn into that world of mysterious creatures, UFOs, and the unexplained. Coincidentally, my birthday falls on Halloween Eve. My parents had purchased a new AM radio as a birthday gift for me. That night I listened to frightening stories about haunted houses, strange creatures, and flying saucers.

Being curious yet skeptical, I was intrigued by these topics and I wanted to know if there was any truth to these accounts. My search began with frequent trips to the local Greensburg library to look for answers, and I became convinced that some of these topics deserved more of my time to further pursue.

Sightings of Unidentified Flying Objects (UFOs) particularly intrigued me. What were those strangely shaped objects seen in the skies over the United States and throughout the world? Had visitors from outside of the Earth interacted with humans, and on occasion landed on our planet? As my research continued, word spread around the school I attended, as well as in my local community, of my interest in such weird matters. Such stories seemed to be brought to my attention, and when the opportunity presented itself, I would speak with local people who claimed to have experienced firsthand encounters with ghosts, UFOs, or anything considered unusual. Quite often, people described their observations of unusually shaped objects that made strange maneuvers in the sky, unlike commercial craft.

Then on December 9, 1965, an unknown object fell from the sky into a wooded area in Mount Pleasant Township, which is only about twelve miles from my hometown. Yet to be identified is the object that brought out the military that night to the village of Kecksburg. Even today I am still gathering information on that now famous 1965 UFO crash case, trying to solve the mystery.

In 1969, I set up a UFO Hotline so that the public could contact me by telephone about any strange incidents. I continue to take calls and receive numerous e-mails concerning current sighting reports. Since I began researching UFO incidents in 1959, I have looked into thousands of alleged UFO observations from across the state. You are about to read reports of some of the most intriguing UFO encounters.

Throughout the years, I founded and directed three research groups made up of many volunteers, including specialists such as scientists, engineers, and technicians. Their purpose was to investigate mysterious events across Pennsylvania. The first group, founded in 1970, was the Westmoreland County UFO Study Group (WCUFOSG). In 1975, the name of the group was changed to the Pennsylvania Center for UFO Research (PCUFOR). In 1981, I founded another group called the Pennsylvania Association for the Study of the Unexplained (PASU) to serve as a statewide clearinghouse for the investigation of unusual events. PASU ceased operations in 1993. I also served as the Pennsylvania State Director for the Mutual UFO Network (MUFON) for many years.

For purposes of geographical clarification, I live in Greensburg, the county seat of Westmoreland County, which is about thirty miles southeast of Pittsburgh, Pennsylvania. The general location is southwestern Pennsylvania. While I primarily receive and investigate odd happenings in the Keystone State, I do occasionally receive sighting reports from Ohio, West Virginia, New York, and Maryland, all of which border Pennsylvania.

Through interviews and research, I realized many years ago that many strange happenings could be explained as originating from natural or man-made sources. Numerous events, however, were highly unusual and quite often not easily explainable. A variety of such accounts are found in this book. Maybe someday we will have the answers as to why these incidents continue to intrude into our lives.

As of this writing, I continue to investigate and document these ongoing incidents from Pennsylvania as an independent researcher. The events that follow are just some of the strange occurrences that have come to my attention over the years. I was personally involved with the investigation of many of the cases mentioned here. These Pennsylvania-based accounts are fascinating, mysterious, and, at times, somewhat scary.

Stan Gordon, 2010

During the early years when I began investigating these cases, a high degree of ridicule at times surrounded the witnesses who reported having such unusual encounters. Even today the ridicule surrounding this subject matters continues, but at a dissipating level. Many of the people involved with these events asked that they not be identified in regard to their experiences. Their wishes have been respected.

Section 1
Encounters with UFOs

Throughout history, man has reported seeing mysterious lights and shapes meandering in the sky. Thousands of reports of UFO sightings are on record from throughout the United States, and from worldwide locations, and the numbers continue to grow. These objects come in numerous shapes, sizes, and colors. Some appear to be solidly constructed craft, while others flit around in the sky like some type of atmospheric life form. On record are numerous accounts of unknown metallic objects pursuing vehicles, hovering near power sources, or landing on the ground, leaving behind various physical traces.

In other landing reports, observers claim to have seen living beings of various descriptions in the vicinity of the object. In many cases I investigated, the UFO was observed at close range. These unknown flying devices range in size from just inches in diameter to hundreds of feet in length. The Air Force officially got out of the UFO investigating business in 1970. That didn't stop the unending appearances of these unknown flying objects. Some very strange and detailed firsthand UFO observations are about to unfold for you in the pages ahead.

Chapter 1
The Early Years

The Kecksburg Incident
December 9, 1965
Kecksburg

This event happened when I was sixteen years old. That evening, I had anticipated tuning into KDKA-AM radio in Pittsburgh to listen to Mike Levine's Contact talk show. His scheduled guest that day was Frank Edwards, a reporter and also an author of some books on "flying saucers," as they commonly called UFOs in those days.

As the broadcast began and Mike introduced Edwards, he indicated what a coincidence it was that, just a short time before, a flurry of calls had been received reporting a widespread sighting of something strange in the sky that was now making local and national news.

It was almost dark when observations were reported at about 4:47 p.m. in the greater Pittsburgh area. Reports of a brilliant fiery object in the sky first began near Ontario, Canada, then over Michigan, Ohio, and into Pennsylvania. Multitudes of witnesses on the ground, as well as aircraft pilots, saw this fiery object move across the sky.

What I learned from years of investigation was that, after moving over the Pittsburgh area, the object continued on into Westmoreland County. As it passed over Greensburg, it continued to track over Route 30 eastward, but then made a turn toward the south. Independent observers watched the object from rural communities such as Margurite, Norvelt, and Mammoth. One witness, the late Randy Overly, was playing outside near Norvelt at the time. He looked to the sky when he heard a hissing sound, and in the distance saw a slow-moving object traveling in his direction. Randy told me that the object was unlike anything he had ever seen before, and it passed only about two hundred feet overhead.

Randy explained to me that the object was brownish-gray in color, shaped like an acorn, and surrounded in a vapor. Also, different colored flames emanated from around the back of the object. Randy said the reason he could see such detail was because the object was moving so slowly. The object continued moving out of sight toward Laurelville.

Not far away, in Mammoth, lived Bill Bulebosh. Bill was in his car adjusting his CB radio when he looked up and saw a fiery object coming from the direction of Norvelt and moving toward Laurelville. Bill ran out to the road and watched as the object in the distance made a turn and then began to travel back toward Kecksburg. The object appeared to be descending, so Bill jumped into his vehicle and drove on a country road to the highest point that overlooked the area. (Interestingly, that road has since been renamed "Meteor Road.")

From his vantage point, he could see bright blue lights flashing down in the woods. Bill knew those woods quite well, since he hunted in that area. He grabbed his flashlight and walked down the embankment. Bill then caught sight of something strange that he would never forget. There, partially imbedded in the ground and only a short distance away, was a strange metallic object.

Bill took safety behind a tree as he watched the object, which was at times emitting something like a blue electrical arcing. The object had some type of strange markings on it. Bill had noticed that some trees in the area had been knocked down, apparently due to the object as it descended. He soon saw other flashlights moving toward that location and he decided to leave. Bill went home and told his wife and young son about what he had found. Bill kept his account quite secretive until 1988, when I received a tip from another source that he had seen the object that fell near Kecksburg. Bill was at the impact site just minutes after the object fell.

It was the year before I met Bill, in August of 1987, that I first learned that a physical object was actually seen on the ground near Kecksburg in 1965. Jim Romansky and his family were walking by the public UFO display I was hosting at the Westmoreland Mall in

Greensburg. One of the tables had some information concerning the Kecksburg event, and one of my associates and another man were discussing the event. Jim overheard some of the conversation and asked if they were talking about that incident.

They acknowledged that they were, and he went on to state that he was in one of the search teams that came across the fallen object that day in 1965. I was away for lunch, so my associates immediately contacted me. I soon met Jim, and he told me the story of what had happened back in 1965, describing in detail what he had seen. He was willing to meet with me on another occasion, but wished to remain anonymous at that point in time.

During the interview, I learned that Jim was not from Kecksburg, but was a member of another volunteer fire company that was called out to assist in a search of the Kecksburg area for a possible downed aircraft. Soon after they entered a wooded area, a call came over a walkie-talkie that the impact site had been found. Jim and his team quickly moved over to that location, and they were quite surprised at what had fallen from the sky. It was unlike anything they had ever seen.

Being a machinist, Jim said that the odd acorn shape of the device was strange, and added that it looked like someone had taken an off-gold-color liquid metal and poured it into an acorn-shaped mold. The object was one solid piece of metal and had no fuselage, wings, seams, or rivets. It appeared to be big enough for a man to stand up inside of it.

From what could be seen of the semi-buried object, Jim estimated it to be about ten to twelve feet or more in length and about eight to ten feet in diameter. At the back of the object was a raised ring section about eight to ten inches wide that Jim called the bumper area. Strange symbols were noted on this ring area. After research, Jim felt they were most similar to ancient Egyptian hieroglyphics.

A mockup of the Kecksburg acorn-shaped UFO is displayed behind the Kecksburg Fire Department, Kecksburg, Pennsylvania. – Copyright: Stan Gordon

As the men stood there for a short time studying the strange contraption, their focus was broken by the sudden appearance of two men in trench coats who spoke sternly to their group. The search team was told to leave immediately because the area was now quarantined. Moments later, military personnel entered through the woods, passing the firemen as they departed.

Jim and the other searchers arrived back at Kecksburg Fire Department truck station and found that there were military personnel and equipment in the area. The arrival of the military was verified by numerous eyewitnesses in different locations around the village that night. Among those who went on record verifying that the military had indeed responded to the scene and utilized the truck station that evening was the late Jim Mayes, who was then the first assistant chief of the Kecksburg Volunteer Fire Department.

On KDKA radio that night, local accounts and news stories about the incident were being reported concerning the fact that something had been seen and had possibly fallen in Westmoreland County near Kecksburg. Later that evening, KDKA-TV broke in with special live reports describing the military arriving and searching for an Unidentified Flying Object that had reportedly fallen into the woods. The question remains even today: what was the fallen object that caused the military to respond so quickly to that small farming community?

Hundreds of people descended into the Kecksburg area that night after hearing the news accounts of the mysterious object falling from the sky. Among the crowds were reporters from Pittsburgh-area radio, TV, and newspaper media, all of whom confirmed a military presence at that location. The witnesses indicated that a great portion of the personnel and equipment appeared to be Army, but others reported Air Force as well.

Later I interviewed others who reported seeing or having had contact with NASA personnel. Also surfacing were reports of men dressed in dark suits who seemed to be working with the military at the scene. Some reports of concern arose from civilians who have publicly acknowledged that soldiers aimed their weapons at them that night in an attempt to make them leave the area near the impact site. What was so important down in the woods that they would threaten to harm civilians, and where did the orders come from to carry out such an operation?

Various witnesses saw a military flatbed tractor trailer truck carrying a large tarpaulin-covered object out of the Kecksburg area about 1:00 a.m. In later years I learned that the object reportedly was taken from there to Lockbourne Air Force base near Columbus, Ohio, for a short stay-over. The truck then continued on to Wright-Patterson Air Force Base near Dayton, Ohio, where the object remained.

Whatever the object was, it appeared to be moving relatively slowly before it fell, made changes in direction, and was reported to drop from the sky in a near controlled landing. So many years later, numerous unanswered questions remain about the event. The main question being, what was the object that fell? During the many years of my investigation into the case, I have been presented with many possible origins of what the object was and where it came from. Among the many theories proposed have been a Soviet satellite, a Soviet ICBM, a missile, a meteorite, a projectile fired from a giant gun in Canada, and a spacecraft from another world.

A number of key witnesses to this case have already passed away. However, still in the area are many people who were involved with the events at Kecksburg that night. They believe that, after so many years, the government should come forth and reveal the truth about what fell into those woods to the citizens of Pennsylvania and the rest of the country.

Rumors persist that photos exist of the fallen object. If you were at Kecksburg that day and have such pictures, or have any information about that event, please get in touch with me.

UFO Hovers above House
Spring 1966
Latrobe

A detailed UFO sighting occurred outside of Latrobe in the spring of 1966. As I began to interview with the woman who reported the sighting, it was obvious that she was still shaken by what had occurred at about 4:00 a.m. that day.

The witness stated that she had been sleeping soundly when suddenly she was awakened by her dog, who was making an odd whining sound. She became alarmed as her dog spun in circles while whining. Her first thought was that her dog was poisoned or dying. She went downstairs to take the animal outside. It was then that her attention was drawn to a silver object hovering only about eighty feet above the roof of her house.

Resembling a huge child's top, the object spun and was encompassed by a reddish glow. On the top of the metallic structure was a vertical projection that could have been an antenna. She listened for sound, but the object was silent. Throughout the event, she became increasingly unnerved, but continued to watch the object for several minutes. As she watched, the hovering object suddenly shot up into the sky at a vertical angle quickly and was lost from her sight in the sky.

While watching the object, the witness tried to yell loudly for someone to come out and look at the object, but realized that she had no voice. Besides losing her voice, she also broke out in a sweat. It took her a little while after the sighting to regain her composure. She then went into the bedroom to awaken her husband to tell him about her experience.

Needless to say, the woman was not happy when her husband started laughing at her and asked if she had seen any little green men. The witness found that she was quite nervous the next day, and she continued to drop things, which was contrary to her usually sure-handed nature. She did tell some close friends as well, and they also ridiculed her. The woman decided to keep her mouth shut and not call the police.

UFO Dives at Car on Highway
August 22, 1966
Adamsburg

One of the first detailed UFO incidents I investigated occurred in the summer of 1966. The date of the incident was August 22. Two women were returning home from Pittsburgh and driving along Route 30, a major highway, near Adamsburg. It was about 9:50 p.m. when they had an unforgettable experience. As the women drove east toward the Adamsburg Cloverleaf area, their attention was drawn to an unusual object hovering over the 500-kilovolt high-tension power lines. The object and the power lines appeared to be almost touching. The observers noticed a glittering effect, or possibly sparking coming from the wires. As the motor vehicle approached the power-line towers, the mysterious aerial object went under the power lines, then moved toward the direction of the car.

Location where UFO incident took place. – Copyright Stan Gordon.

The two women ducked their heads, as it appeared that the object was about to hit their car. The car was traveling in the right lane of the highway, and the object entered that lane as it passed overhead. No sound could be heard from the object. The women reported its size to be about the length of an MG sports car.

The object appeared to be a dark color, and was oblong in shape. The body of the craft appeared to be about two to three feet thick. The front structure seemed flat, and the shape rounded out toward the back into a type of tail. Deep grooves appeared to be on the surface of the object.

As soon as the women arrived at their home, they called the state police. Soon after the encounter, I interviewed the driver and found her to be still quite upset. Later I learned that she had nightmares about the occurrence for three nights after it happened. This woman never believed in UFOs until that evening in 1966.

Chapter 2
Varied Shapes

Cigar-Shaped Object Hovers over Mall
August 12, 1986
Monroeville

Two persons employed in a motel near Monroeville Mall observed a strange object at about 8:30 a.m. on the morning of August 12, 1986. When the object was first observed, it was hovering over a group of trees behind the mall. After hovering, the object moved over the tree line in the direction of the mall. It came to a complete stop directly over the Horne's store roof at an estimated height of two hundred feet. After hovering there for about ten seconds, it moved to the right at a rapid pace, stopped suddenly, and once again hovered over the roof of the front entrance.

After another ten seconds, it shot quickly to the right and hovered over another store roof.

It then moved around the mall and could no longer be seen. The witnesses stated that the object hovered over large air-conditioning units on the roof. The object was approximately four hundred feet from the observers and was seen for an estimated three minutes or more.

The object itself was elongated in shape, similar to a cigar, and appeared solid. One witness told me that it was "fat and rounded out." It was such a bright shiny silver color that it hurt the observers' eyes. The object was about the size of three school buses in length, and no sound was associated with the sighting. Each of the witnesses attempted to locate others who may have seen the object, but stopped when they began to be ridiculed. The weather was clear and comfortable at the time of the observation.

Later the same day at about 2:30 p.m., a similar object was seen about twenty miles south of Monroeville Mall near the town of Mt.

Pleasant. It was a nice clear day, and the temperature was about 75 degrees when a man was driving on Route 31 west. He stopped and got a clear look at the airborne object that he described as an elongated metallic object hovering over the area. The edges of the object seemed to be outlined in black, while the rest of the object appeared metallic. The witness lost sight of the object after it moved over some trees.

Additionally I received a phone call from an unknown female who described seeing apparently the same object in the same area. In the weeks to follow, this general area had a number of additional sightings.

Daylight Cigar Hovers Low over Trees
August 1986
New Alexandria

Late in August 1986 near New Alexandria, a businessman was traveling north on Route 981 at about 2:30 p.m. when he observed a large cigar-shaped object about fifty feet above the ground over some trees. He described the object as being metallic silver in color and quite shiny, and he estimated it to be about two hundred feet long. Within about five minutes, he drove a short distance and located some other friends to tell them about what he had seen.

He then got into a four-wheel drive vehicle and returned to the top of a ridge to look toward the area where he last saw the object. Upon returning, he could not initially see the object or any evidence of it being there. He then looked across the valley and saw the object over another knoll about two miles away, watching as it dropped down below the tree line. The object had no markings on it and was completely silent. The object hovered low for a minute, then it began to slowly glide off between the trees and the hill and was soon gone. The Loyalhanna Dam was only about a mile away.

Giant Disc-Shaped Object above House
October 1986
Harrisburg

In early October 1986 in Harrisburg, Dauphin County, a witness had a close-range UFO sighting during the early morning hours. At 4:15 a.m., the witness had awakened in her home when she noticed a brilliant light at the window. Upon looking out the window, the light was seen to be emitted from a huge, bright white, disc-shaped object that hovered over the area at an altitude of about fifty feet. The object had some type of cloud or mist surrounding it.

The diameter of the huge object encompassed an area of five homes simultaneously, or about half a football field. As the object continually rotated counterclockwise, the woods and backyard behind her home became brightly illuminated. The object made no sound as it hovered for about one minute. It then moved back in the direction from which it came. Soon after the sighting, the woman's young son awoke and she described what she had seen to him. A short time later he also saw the object, but it was farther away in the distance and soon was gone from sight.

Couple Watches UFO Change Shape
August 8, 1987
Clarion County

It was about 9:00 p.m. on August 8, 1987, when a couple was riding down a country road to a friend's home in Clarion County. On the left side of the road about seventy-five yards into the woods, they observed a strange object that at first gave the impression of being on fire. The object appeared to be about fifty feet above the ground and rising upward.

When the UFO was first observed, it looked like a giant kite. One witness told me that it was like a long rod with two square wings and a glowing, luminous orange color, as though it was on fire. The other witness said it reminded him more of a massive amount of electric arc welding. As the object rose toward the sky, it appeared to be changing its physical form. The object moved up to about one hundred feet over the treetops.

The couple lost sight of it for just seconds, and when they got to a clearing in the woods, they had an unobstructed view. They immediately noticed that the object was physically different. It now looked like a brilliant orange-colored, egg-shaped structure with numerous small orange-colored lights around its perimeter, as well as through the center section. The color of the object was brighter in the center area. One witness stated that, while the color was intensely bright, it was not so bright that it hurt her eyes. The object was about twenty feet long and made no sound.

The object seemed to hover momentarily, then it moved forward toward the direction of the car. The couple followed the object down the road a couple of miles. The object seemed to keep pace with their vehicle as though they were watching each other. The couple decided to pull off the road and drive into a field to continue to watch the object. Suddenly the object shot straight up into the sky at an incredible speed, turning into an orange dot of light and moving so fast that the couple could hardly see it leaving.

They continued on to their friend's house and told them about what they had seen. They sat there, discussed the sighting, and drew some sketches. They also mentioned that while sitting outside that evening they heard jet aircraft flying overhead, which was unusual for that area. The entire sighting lasted about five minutes. The witnesses decided to call the police authorities two days after the incident. The police referred the call to my UFO Hotline.

Two Huge Triangular Objects in Formation
February 13, 1995
Westmoreland County

The sky was clear on the evening of February 12, 1995. It was nearly 8:00 p.m. when the witness looked through a window into the northeast sky and saw a strange pattern of lights that moved toward the northwest. Having many years of experience as an aircraft pilot, he knew that this light pattern was not the normal navigational lighting on an airplane.

He grabbed his binoculars and ran outside to get a better look at the lights. His first thoughts were that it was a KC-97 tanker that was refueling military jets, but the spacing of lights, color, and pattern soon ruled that out. The witness soon had a better view of the objects, and realized that they were something that he had never seen before.

What he was watching were two huge, solid, triangular-shaped objects that blocked the view of the stars as they passed over. The silent objects were observed moving from horizon to horizon, and crossed the sky in about fifteen minutes. The man estimated that they were between eight and ten thousand feet in altitude. The objects stayed in perfect formation but quite a distance apart as they crossed the sky.

Each object had a dim white light at the front. The five lights on the rear of the objects were unusual. The first was a bright red pulsating light on the left corner, then one dim white light, a large bright white-orange light in the center, then another dim white light, and finally ending with a white light.

The objects were not moving on a typical flight path over the area. Soon after seeing the two huge objects pass out of sight, the witness contacted an FAA Flight Service Station, asking if any military flights or blimps were passing through the area. He was informed that this was not the case. That facility contacted the control tower at Greater Pittsburgh Airport, which reportedly was unable to obtain a radar contact on the two objects.

The man was then directed to contact me about his encounter. In ensuing interviews, he related that he was quite amazed at what he had seen, considering his ten years of experience as a pilot and familiarity with aircraft. Previously he had never believed the accounts he had heard about UFO sightings. The events of that night had changed his mind, though.

The witness sent me a statement about his experience, which included the following, "I do not care to see them again. Please do not think I am crazy, for I am not. I have been a pilot for ten years and I have seen all manner of aircraft, civil and military, and have never seen anything like this. This was a damn strange experience that I don't want to repeat on the ground or in flight."

Gold-Colored, Cigar-Shaped Object Approaches Car
August 1, 1995
Forbes Road

It was about 10:30 p.m. on August 1, 1995, when two men driving through a rural location near Forbes Road had an encounter with a UFO that they told me, "scared the hell out of us." The men were driving toward the end of a road and coming into a clearing when the incident took place.

Suddenly in front of them appeared what at first they thought was a helicopter or some other aircraft. After they continued to observe the craft, they soon realized that this was something much more unusual. This object was elongated like a cigar, about one hundred fifty feet in length, and was a solid object, gold in color. As the object approached their car, the color of the object began to intensify.

The cigar-shaped craft began to emit brilliant flashes of gold-orange light that looked similar to lightning flashes. When these light emissions occurred, they would illuminate the area that surrounded the object. The men listened intently but heard no sound. The two observers watched the object hover nearby for about five minutes.

They then decided to flash their headlights at the object to see if they could provoke any response.

That did indeed cause the object to react. The mysterious object began to approach the direction of their car. When the object reached a distance of about eighty feet away, the two frightened men quickly sped out of the area. I was told that they were nearly underneath the object as they made their getaway. They then watched as the object moved off across the sky.

Chapter 3
Massive UFOs

"Cruise Ship" in the Sky Seen by Many
February 10, 1988
Cambria and Somerset Counties

Several individuals reported seeing an elongated object over about a ten-mile area on the evening of February 10, 1988, between 7:45 and 8:30 p.m. The area of activity encompassed locations bordering Somerset and Cambria counties.

The first report was near the village of Blough. Three cars were on a road between Hooversville and Pretoria when the driver of the first car noticed "a huge object the size of a house" hovering just above the water on the other side of a nearby bridge. The object appeared solid, was gray in color, and was estimated to be about sixty feet long. It had at least two rows of lights—red on the top and green on the bottom of the object, all of which remained steady and did not blink. The object itself hovered approximately fifty feet above the water and was within one hundred feet of the witnesses.

The first driver swerved off the road three times while trying to drive and see what was going on in the sky. He finally stopped his car, and the other vehicles behind him stopped also. From this point, they could see the object still hovering and could hear only a slight humming noise. The object suddenly turned on several bright white spotlights from its lower left side and directed them toward a nearby wooded area. The lights seemed to reach only the top of the trees, and did not penetrate the area below. In the distance, another smaller object appeared and began to move in a circular pattern over the woods. At this point the cars left the area, but they were still able to see the object higher in the sky from a distance.

At about 8:00 p.m., another man was traveling south on Route 219 near the vicinity of the McNally Bridge. As he drove onto the bridge, the object rose from beneath the bridge to his right, reached about the same level as the bridge, and was around one hundred fifty feet from the observer. He noted that other cars traveling in the area also stopped to observe the object. He described the object as being about fifty to sixty feet long and about twenty-five feet wide. It looked like a football and had a shiny metallic covering. From the front of the object, five or six bright "laser-type lights" were emitted outward. One smaller red light shone at the rear of the object. The witness was amazed that this object could hover with no apparent sound, wings, or propellers. After a short time, the object began to move off into the distance. As it left, the lights seemed to diminish in brightness.

Another witness on this evening was driving up a hill on a back road near the Davidsville area when at about 8:20 p.m. an object that he described as "a small cruise ship in the sky" passed directly in front of him at an estimated distance of twenty feet away. He then stopped his truck and turned off the heater and the radio.

The object was described as being fifty feet long and wide, and, once again, was shaped like a football with tapered ends easily visible on the solid surface. The object had numerous lights of various colors, with some blinking and others remaining steady. Baffled by this sight, the witness decided to drive the remaining twenty yards to the top of the hill where he could get a better view of this silent object. By the time he reached this location where the object had been hovering seconds before, it had now moved a considerable distance from him, which he estimated to be about two miles away, and was now higher in the sky.

Rectangular UFO Causes House to Vibrate
Winter, 1988
Feasterville

It was about 2:30 one winter morning in 1988, when a woman was awakened from sleep after she felt a cold draft. When she went to the window to make sure it was closed, she noticed that the sky was cloudy and no stars were visible. However, something odd in the sky did catch her attention. What she saw was an object that resembled something like two very bright street lights that were attached to a larger construct. The movement of the sky object was odd in that it would move back and forth, then upward, and in a clockwise and then counterclockwise pattern. The witness continued to watch this strange activity for about fifteen minutes.

The object then appeared to flip over, make a sudden direction change, and move slowly but directly toward the roof of her house. The witness bent down, looking up from her window to see the roof area better to view the object that she could not believe she was seeing. At that point the dark solid object then appeared to be only about forty feet above the roof.

She described the object as huge, dark gray in color, and shaped like a huge solid rectangle. Areas on the bottom of the structure appeared to have black patches, which the witness conjectured may have been doors or some other structure. A total of three lights could be seen on the craft, two green, and one red, and none were flashing. The object itself did not appear to make any sound, but caused a vibration effect while it was overhead.

When the object moved above the house, she felt strong vibrations in her home. The windows started to rattle, the window shades began to flop around, and even the bed reportedly shook. The dog was quiet and only barked once as the object left. The woman thought about awakening her sleeping husband, but didn't want to take her eyes off of the object. The object then moved off across the sky and was not seen again.

The witness was quite upset after this close encounter. During the interview, she provided a detailed account of the event. In her efforts to find an explanation for the aerial object, she placed a call to the Willow Grove Naval Air Station and filed a report on the mysterious flying object. I later talked with an officer at that base concerning the incident.

Additionally I filed a Freedom of Information Act (FOIA) request for a copy of the report that was taken concerning the sighting, and subsequently received a copy of that incident report. The officer who had spoken with the witness and wrote the report noted in the comments about the sighting that the witness "seemed to be reasonable and rational about her observations but at the same time concerned about what she saw."

Huge Rumbling Triangle Returns
October 12, 1995
Centre County

In February 1992, a multiple-witness UFO sighting occurred over widespread and some well-populated areas around Williamsport, Pennsylvania. Numerous people reported seeing large triangular or boomerang-shaped objects that generally moved quite slowly and produced a loud rumbling sound that actually shook the homes in some areas.

It now seems that a similar object created a similar scenario on the evening of October 12, 1995, in Centre County. The sightings occurred about 8:15 p.m. in a rural area of the county. Witnesses reported hearing a loud sound, like a train approaching, and they began to feel a strong vibration. As the sound seemed to get closer and louder, their house began to shake. One witness reported that she was afraid the house was going to collapse.

The occupants of the home ran outside to discover what was causing the sound and were amazed to see a large object overhead that they described as a rounded triangle of grayish-silver color. At the bottom of the object was an unlit, almost circular shape. The back of the device was described as having a somewhat rounded triangular shape with eight rectangular lights across its back.

When witnesses first observed the object, it was hovering at a height of about one hundred feet above them and about one hundred feet away from them. No markings were visible on the surface of the object. They reported a total of eight lights that consisted of six orange lights flanked by one red light on each end. The size of the object was estimated at two hundred feet wide and one hundred feet long. The object was observed for about five minutes as it passed slowly out of sight, but the sound could be heard in the distance.

Witnesses reported their dogs seemed upset during the incident. Also noted was a power loss to all the digital clocks in the house. A local airport reportedly received many calls concerning the object from the Beech Creek and Blanchard areas. One witness I interviewed was a pilot who had observed a triangular formation of lights from the ground. He was in his house at the time when he heard the loud rumbling sound and looked in a southerly direction, where he observed the unusual pattern of lights. It is my understanding that similar reports occurred that same night near Williamsport.

Chapter 4
Encounters in Densely
Populated Areas

Quite often, those skeptical of the existence of legitimate UFO encounters often bring up what they believe to be factual information: that these incidents are only reported by observers in rural communities. While many UFO incidents are in fact reported from rural locations, numerous other UFO sightings have occurred over highly populated or well-traveled areas as well. In Pennsylvania, UFO encounters have been reported around Pittsburgh, Philadelphia, Harrisburg, and even on the Pennsylvania Turnpike.

UFO Visits Pittsburgh Suburb
May 17, 1989
Pittsburgh (Squirrel Hill)

One UFO encounter over a densely populated area occurred just before 3:00 a.m. on the morning of May 17, 1989, in Squirrel Hill, a heavily populated suburb of Pittsburgh. Two young women, ages twenty-seven and twenty-eight, had stopped at a local restaurant.

After leaving the restaurant, they were driving down Murray Avenue and made a right onto Beacon Street. They were in the middle of the block approaching Wightman Street when the women suddenly observed a large object hovering above the intersection of Beacon and Wightman. The driver of the car was so shocked that she stopped and got out of the vehicle to look directly at it. The women's first impression was that they were seeing a blimp, but as they watched, they realized that this object was more elongated and was brightly lit, almost luminous white in color.

The witnesses were interviewed by PASU investigator Evelyn Schurman. The observers mentioned that, toward the bottom of the object, three large red lights appeared to be connected together. These lights were positioned from about the center area and extended to the right side of the craft. The lights were flashing, but seemed to be generally in the "on" cycle when observed. Some other sections of the object were irregularly shaped, but not as bright as other sections. The object that hovered over the area for about three to four minutes and made no sound. Some indentations were also noted in the craft.

Several times the object changed from its hovering position, backed away from that location, and then remained motionless again. At one point the witnesses noticed clouds drifting past the object. The object did not move off across the sky, but seemed to just vanish in front of their eyes. The women were so disturbed by their experience that they contacted the Pittsburgh police, Zone 6, who took a report on the strange incident. The story was later picked up the local news.

I checked the weather conditions at Greater Pittsburgh and Allegheny County airports for the time of the UFO observation, and no existing weather events could account for what was reported. The control tower at Greater Pittsburgh Airport reported that nothing odd had appeared on radar, and no takeoffs or landings had occurred around the observation time.

It was later learned that another young woman and her date were parked on a back road at nearby Schenley Park at about 3:00 a.m. when they also had a strange event occur. The fellow in the car noticed that a figure dressed completely in white was walking ahead. The man thought that this was somewhat strange. The woman in the car experienced something more unusual. She saw a shadow that seemed to glide past their car, which blocked some of the light that was coming into the vehicle.

UFO Hovers over Pittsburgh Bridge
July 14, 1995
Pittsburgh

Three witnesses reported seeing a strange object hovering over the Homestead High Level Bridge in a suburb of Pittsburgh. The observation occurred at about 2:00 a.m. on July 14, 1995. The object was described as being larger in size than a blimp and covered with hundreds of colored lights. The lighting colors were quite unusual and were said to be purple-blue and pinkish-red. The object was said to have hovered over the bridge for about a minute before ascending into the sky at a high rate of speed and quickly disappearing from sight.

There have been a number of UFO sightings reported in the Pittsburgh area.

Chapter 5
Physical Effects

In this chapter I have included examples of both physical effects to the environment as well as to individuals. A long history of witnesses have reported various effects when in close proximity to a UFO. Historically in some instances, also reported were localized power losses when a UFO was observed. In some instances unknown objects in close proximity to moving vehicles caused power loss, headlights dimming, or interference with the radio reception.

Some observers have also experienced physiological effects. In some cases witnesses have reported eye and skin irritation or burns. Some reported temporary paralysis as well as tingling effects. In one case a witness reported loss of hearing from a UFO emitting a high-pitched sound.

Did a Giant UFO Cause Power Outage?
September 3, 1987
Greensburg

It was the evening of September 3, 1987, when a strange aerial object appeared low in the sky over a busy shopping area on Route 30, east of Greensburg. It was about 8:30 p.m. when a group of people, including law enforcement officers, standing near the movie theater complex behind the Greengate Mall, saw something unusual in the sky. Looking toward the west about a quarter of a mile away, they saw an object approaching as it crossed over Route 30, moving over high-tension power lines and toward the West Penn Power substation. The station was located behind the Greengate Apartments and across the highway from the mall.

Their first impression was that it was a blimp, but their perception soon changed. The object was immense in size. The cigar-shaped object was estimated to be about three hundred feet in length. One witness stated that, to him, the object looked to be the length of two

Goodyear blimps, and about as thick as one blimp. The elongated construct appeared to be a solid craft with a silver or dull gray surface. Moving at about fifty to sixty miles an hour, no sound was discernible. The object was quite low and moving about three hundred feet above the ground. The entire object had many brilliant blinking lights that were white in color, flanked by bright flashing red lights on each end.

Artist depiction of UFO incident near Greensburg, Pennsylvania.
Drawing by Robert McCurry

The observers continued to watch the object as it moved in a smooth horizontal path. Then the object suddenly made a maneuver that stunned them. The football-field sized object suddenly turned vertically in the sky. For a moment the power in the area suddenly went off in the Greengate Mall and the surrounding area. The view of the object was blocked for a short time by the trees, but when it was seen again, it had returned to its original horizontal stance.

It was later that same evening when a major power failure occurred in the annex of the Greengate Mall at the theater complex. It was my understanding that the theater area received its power from the power substation near which the object had passed. A crew from West Penn Power arrived on the scene and discovered that all three of the main fuses located in the feed line had been blown. It was also my understanding in speaking with some electrical engineers at the time that this sort of event, when several fuses blow simultaneously, was quite unusual. What this object was, and where it went to, remains unknown.

A Numbing Effect
November 13, 1987
Greensburg

On November 13, 1987, at 10:00 p.m., two witnesses reported a huge object covered with lights moving from the Manor area toward Jeanette. About fifteen minutes later, a woman taking a walk noticed a large object coming straight down the country road at an altitude of about one hundred feet, just clearing the tops of the nearby trees.

The location of the sighting was off Route 130 near the Greensburg Country Club. The witness at first thought that this was a large airplane in trouble and was preparing to make an emergency landing on the golf course. As she stood and watched the large object pass directly to her left, she realized that the object was something quite unusual.

The witness estimated the object to be about one hundred feet long and with a definite rectangular-box shape. It appeared to be a metallic gray color and had sharply defined edges. A bright red stripe ran across the width of the structure, and red and green lights could be seen on the object.

The witness heard a loud high-pitched sound, unlike that of a normal aircraft engine. Then the witness watched as the object kept slowly moving off in the distance, but it seemed to just suddenly disappear. This witness reported that, a short time after the incident, the entire left side of her face had no feeling, as if she'd had an injection of Novocaine.

UFO Causes Radio Interference
September 28, 1988
Derry Township

A utility company supervisor was driving south toward Route 982 at 6:45 a.m. on September 28, 1988. He had driven this road many times but never had an experience like what was about to take place. He was about four to five hundred feet away from reaching Route 982 in Derry Township when he began to notice a loud scratchy noise on his radio, which affected both the AM and FM radio bands. He then turned off the vehicle's radio.

About the same time, his two-way business radio began to have interference also, so he turned the volume down on that unit. Then he noticed something more unusual with his communications equipment. The witness also carried a VHF pocket pager that was turned off at the time. Nonetheless, it began to emit a loud squealing noise. He checked the unit and turned it on and off, but it continued to squeal.

As the man approached the Route 982 South intersection, he saw a strange hovering light about two hundred feet ahead of him that was around fifty feet off the ground. The object was about twelve to fifteen feet in diameter. It was described as a bright white ball divided into three sections and what seemed to be two bars went vertically up the entire length of the light. The light began to pace the truck for a short distance, keeping an equal distance from it, before he lost sight of it near a wooded area. Once it was out of sight, the radio interference ceased.

Chapter 6
Photographic Evidence

Luminous Hovering Object Photographed
January 3, 2007
Youngwood

It was lucky that one of three passengers traveling in a car outside of Youngwood had purchased a new cell phone with a "night mode" setting in the camera function just days before. That person had no idea that the cell phone camera would produce evidence that they had all seen something strange in the sky.

It was the evening of January 3, 2007, and it was exactly 8:58 p.m. as noted on the photo-date display of the camera. These three people were traveling down a rural location outside of Youngwood. It was a nice clear night and many stars were visible. Suddenly the attention of the three people was drawn to a large luminous object that appeared quite low in the sky, and was either hovering or moving slowly.

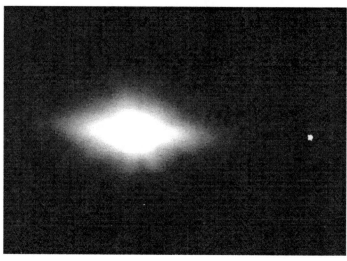

UFO photograph taken near Youngwood, Pennsylvana. Used with permission of the owner.

Upon seeing the object, the woman yelled out, "What the hell is that light? Why is it so low?" As the car continued down the road, they noticed the moon to their left, so they could rule out the other object as being the moon. One witness described the object to me as a diamond shape, or "oval shaped with a hump at the top and bottom." The entire object was surrounded with a glowing effect. The object was much larger and brighter than any of the stars observed in the clear night sky. The object was silent and quite large in size.

As the object moved slowly and low in the air, they lost sight of it at times since some houses or trees were blocking it from view. They moved down the road farther to a location where they had a better view of the glowing diamond-shaped object, which seemed to be motionless. As they moved forward to another location, they stopped their vehicle at the point where they had a clear unobstructed view of the hovering object. It was then that the window was rolled down on the driver's side, the cell phone camera was switched on to the night-mode setting, and with a click, the woman took one photo of the strange object.

The lady in the car immediately checked the telephone video monitor to see if the image had been captured. The three people were quite excited when they saw that they had indeed obtained a picture of the mysterious glowing object. It was just seconds after the picture was taken that the woman looked back to where the object had been, but it was no longer visible. The other observers were unsure what happened to the object, as it seemed to have suddenly disappeared from sight. One witness described it to me this way, "It was there, then it wasn't there." The object was under observation for about three to four minutes.

Odd-Shaped Object Photographed on the Ground
September 1, 1995
Penn

A man driving near Penn and returning home at about 3:30 a.m. on the morning of September 1, 1995, was surprised when he noticed something on the railroad tracks. He saw ahead in the distance what appeared to be a brilliant gold-yellow light that seemed to be resting on the ground or just above the railroad tracks to the right side of the road.

Having never seen anything like that on his many trips through the area, he pulled his car off the road to get a better glimpse at the spectacle. The man stopped his car and exited the vehicle, walking toward the light source. He stopped about thirty feet away, trying to figure out just what he was seeing.

When I interviewed this man about what he saw, he was still having difficulty trying to describe the object. The man said that the object itself was about twenty feet high and almost as wide as the railroad tracks. It was the shape that was difficult to explain. According to the eyewitness, it looked like a capital letter W, but with an extra extension.

Since he had just returned from vacation, he luckily had a Polaroid camera in his vehicle that still had some film. After he ran back to his car and grabbed the camera, he took it back to the location where the object rested. The man was beginning to feel uneasy, but he took one picture of the mysterious object before he left the site. As the man drove down the road, the object remained at the same location.

I was shown the Polaroid photo of the unknown object. While not much detail could be seen in the night photo, I was able make out a gold-colored object with the shape the witness described. That same area has a long history of numerous UFO encounters.

Chapter 7
Dangerous Situations

Huge Metallic Craft Blocks Roadway
August 30, 1983
Derry

It was just about midnight on August 30, 1983, when a man traveling on Route 217 toward Derry had not one, but a series of three encounters with a UFO on the same roadway. The witness was a businessman driving north at the Kingston Cutoff, headed toward Derry. It was a nice evening, the temperature was about seventy degrees, and it was clear and dry.

As the man drove down a hill, his attention was drawn to a series of amber lights that suddenly appeared overhead through his windshield. The driver quickly found himself underneath a huge, solid round object that seemed to hover about forty to sixty feet above him. The bottom of the object appeared flat. The man became fearful due to the close approach of this unknown object, and the strange sound that it was emitting only added to the man's anxiety.

The loud sound was intense and penetrating, having a strong bass tone that actually vibrated throughout his body in a "whoop-whoop" pattern. The man soon realized that this object was tremendous in size, engulfing both sides of the roadway, and blocking his view of the sky. The witness estimated the width to be about two to three hundred feet in diameter.

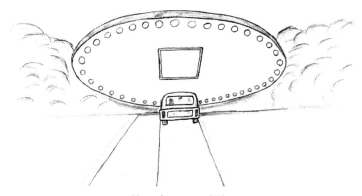

Huge object over vehicle.
Drawing by Robert McCurry

The object appeared to be battleship gray in color, but seemed to have a bluish tinge as well. While the bottom area was flat, another area of about forty to sixty feet seemed to be either square or slightly rectangular and was outlined in black. This gave the witness the impression that this could be an entryway or door, which could possibly either slide or drop open.

The entire bottom perimeter of the round object was covered in amber-colored lights, each producing a soft yet bright glow. These amber lights did not seem to give off any reflected light to the surrounding area. The lights themselves were estimated to range from about nine to thirteen inches in diameter and were not flashing. A pattern to the lighting could also be discerned, with each light spaced evenly at a distance of about four to five feet. Between the amber lights and the edge of the object, there was a distance of about three feet.

The motorist became frightened as the object hovered overhead, and he accelerated to speeds up to eighty-five miles per hour to get away from the huge device. He continued down the road, then moments later, the object overtook his vehicle again and, once more, hovered overhead.

The thumping sound was reverberating through his body. The object did not sway like a helicopter, but appeared to be motionless about forty feet or so above him, as it had been before. For the second time, the man sped down the road trying to escape from the huge mysterious craft. The object moved parallel with the movement of his vehicle.

Then only a short distance farther down the roadway, the object once again positioned itself just as closely as before over the frightened man. The sound continued to vibrate and unnerve the witness. The object finally moved off in the distance.

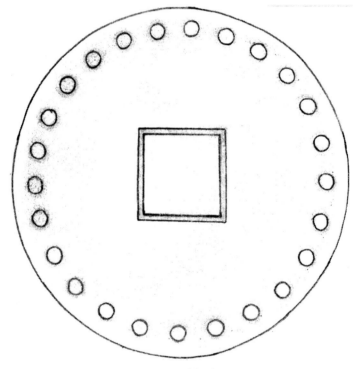

Bottom view of the object.
Drawing by Robert McCurry

The object played its cat-and-mouse game with this driver three times total over a short stretch of roadway. The witness told me that, during the last two encounters, the object seemed so low that he thought it was going to hit some roof racks on his vehicle. He felt claustrophobic each time he was under the huge object, feeling closed in even though he was on an open road. He described the experience as similar to the experience of driving into a large underground lighted parking lot.

After arriving home, he was still upset about what had happened. He then called the Latrobe police to report what had happened. They referred him to contact me via my UFO Hotline.

Did a UFO Cause a Train Derailment?
July 1, 1988
Sharpsburg (Pittsburgh suburb)

It's really not that unusual to hear a news report concerning a train going off the railroad tracks. But when such an accident reportedly has a UFO involved with the mishap, the event becomes more interesting. That's exactly what happened near Pittsburgh in 1988. The story even made the local news.

It was about 3:30 a.m. on the morning of July 1, 1988, when thirty-five cars of a Conrail train derailed near the Pittsburgh suburb of Sharpsburg. A diesel engine had been pulling the railroad cars, which were loaded with welded railings. As the train was traveling through the area, it suddenly left the tracks. Police officers quickly responded to the scene of the accident and were approached by a man who had a strange story to tell them.

What I learned from one of the police officers was that the fellow related how he was sitting in his car in the parking lot of the Waterworks Mall and saw the train approaching the area. At that point he also noticed something unusual. His attention was attracted to a luminous object in the sky that was approaching from the direction of Route 28. The bright object passed over the mall area and then moved toward the train.

The man told police that, at the same time the "spaceship" was above the train, he noticed a great amount of sparking suddenly occurring underneath the train cars. Moments later the train went off the tracks. The police officers said that the man appeared serious and he had not been drinking.

A few other individuals were out and about in the general area during that early morning hour. One man was pumping gas when he saw an object in the sky that he assumed was a helicopter, but then realized that it made no sound. The official explanation from Conrail was that the wreck was caused by a split rail.

Chapter 8
Government Interest?

Was Video of Hovering UFO Confiscated?
January 24, 1987
Pittsburgh Region

In late January 1987, a UFO incident came to my attention from several callers on my UFO Hotline. One of the informants was a reporter from the Pittsburgh area who had been trying to follow up on this report. As I began to investigate the incident, it appeared that some of the individuals involved were reluctant to discuss what had occurred. I learned that the witnesses' hesitation stemmed from their concern that, if they talked about what they saw, their jobs could be in jeopardy.

The location of this UFO incident reportedly occurred in the greater Pittsburgh area at the site of a manufacturing complex that had some government affiliation. It was during the early morning hours of January 24, 1987, when quite a number of employees reportedly observed a large luminous object hovering low over the facility for an extensive period of time. One description of the object was that its shape was like an orange cut in half, or like a dome. It was about one hundred feet in diameter and made no sound. The object was revolving and tilted at times, as it illuminated the area.

During its visit the UFO was also said to have hovered near a security guard station. One guard reportedly was able to obtain a company video camcorder, and taped over fifteen minutes of video footage of this object hovering around the site. It was reported that, the day after the incident, an executive of the company arrived at the location and took possession of the videotape showing the object. That official was also said to have gathered the employees together to discuss what had occurred, and reportedly told them not to talk about what had happened. He was said to have told these people that, as far as the company was concerned, they had only seen a navigational light on a radio tower.

To follow up with the investigation, I contacted the facility directly. I received a reply that the videotape was reviewed and nothing unusual was seen on it. The videotape was then recycled for further use. Was there a cover-up to hide evidence of a real UFO visit? We will probably never know for sure.

Government Still Investigating UFOs?

For many years the United States Air Force officially investigated UFO sightings reported by the public. Project Blue Book officially terminated its investigations into these sightings in 1970. Incidents such as the following, though, suggest that our government continues to take such sightings seriously.

Did Military Jets Chase UFOs over Pennsylvania?
August and October 1989 in Butler County
November 1989 in Westmoreland County

On occasion I have received reports from the public concerning sightings of UFOs that appeared to be pursued by military jets. Three such incidents occurred within a four-month time span during 1989. The first report was after 9:00 p.m. on the night of August 31.

Two observers in a rural area of Butler County watched a bright, mushroom-shaped light hover over a field for about ten minutes. The object made no sound, and apparently two smaller red illuminated objects emerged from the larger object before all three moved out of the area. Within a short time two military-type jets appeared on the scene and circled the area for about half an hour before departing. On this same night a series of UFO sightings were reported from Westmoreland, Cambria, Blair, and Somerset counties as well. The Butler County area had been experiencing a series of UFO sightings since January of that year.

On the night of October 28, 1989, another witness, also from Butler County, reported that about 10:00 p.m., he was walking outside and enjoying the clear sky when he observed a slow-moving light as it approached from the northeast. The man noticed that his dog was carrying on and became upset as the light approached. The light was making a flittering movement similar to how a bug moves in flight, and it appeared to be only a couple hundred feet above the ground. The light was attached to a football-shaped object that had red and yellow lights on the back section. After a short time the light ascended into the sky and moved out of sight.

Within a short time the witness was startled to hear jet engines roar overhead while other lights simultaneously appeared in the same general area of the sky. The witness stated that he observed what appeared to be a total of about fifteen military jets move into the area. The jets were in a single-file formation, following one after the other at about fifteen-second intervals, as though in quick pursuit of the strange light.

Never had the witness seen so many military jets in the area before. They approached from the direction of Ohio. This observer contacted the Air Force base near Pittsburgh to report this sighting, and he was referred to my UFO Hotline number.

The third such sighting in this series occurred on November13, 1989, at 10:05 p.m. A person near Greensburg in Westmoreland County looked up into the clear night sky and saw three bright star-like objects grouped together, their lights blinking on and off. He watched them for about ten minutes as they moved relatively slowly across the sky. Then they began to move at a faster rate of speed. As they moved off, they split apart, and two of the lights moved eastward.

The third light then moved toward the west. Next, he noticed that a jet with a contrail was moving at a high rate of speed and pursuing the object. The jet did not seem to be able to catch up with the object at that point. The witness watched the pursuit until they were out of sight.

This man had never seen anything like this before and quickly called me to report the sighting. While the Air Force and other government agencies tell us that they no longer investigate UFO cases, incidents such as these make us wonder if that is really the case. It is likely that the military jets were scrambled from a base in Ohio.

Chapter 9
Widespread Sighting of UFOs

The 1986 Labor Day Weekend UFO Incident
August 31, 1986
New Stanton

It was Labor Day weekend in 1986, and many people were traveling across the highways in Pennsylvania. On the evening of August 31, something strange was observed in the sky, involving numerous witnesses. I first became aware of this incident the next morning after a series of early morning phone calls to my UFO Hotline number. Several individuals who had witnessed the event the previous night wanted to find out what exactly they had seen.

One couple had been traveling southbound on new Route 119 near what was then the Volkswagen assembly plant near New Stanton. About 9 p.m., they both observed a series of lights that gave them the impression that an aircraft was dropping from the sky and in the midst of making an emergency landing. The lighting pattern observed by the man was of four large, bright green lights in a row, which gave the impression of being connected along a fuselage.

His wife said, from her position, she was able to see the four lights in a row at the bottom. She noted a second level consisting of two bright lights, one yellow and one green, and also a third level with only one light. As the object got lower in the sky, it appeared to turn and level out. The entire observation lasted for about thirty seconds; they could hear no sound.

The couple lost sight of the lights as they went around a curve. In the vicinity where the lights had vanished, they suddenly observed a brilliant fire at the top of the embankment along the highway. The hillside was located between a stretch of Old Route 119 and new Route 119. The couple pulled over and the husband ran out. Thinking that an aircraft had crashed, the man climbed about fifty feet to the top of the hill.

They were not the only travelers to see what they initially thought was an aircraft going down. Other drivers approaching the area from both directions also stopped to render assistance. Another man in a brown van ran across the highway with canoe oars in hand and approached the fire scene. He immediately began to put out the flames. The fire was confined to about a nine-foot circular area, with flames reaching about four feet in the air.

Embankment along Route 119 where fire was seen.
Photograph by George E. Lutz

A couple of feet away another three-foot area was also burning. The fires were quickly extinguished. What started the fires was not apparent, and a search of the area found no evidence of a downed aircraft. Some people contacted local emergency agencies to report a possible airplane crash, and a local fire department responded at the scene.

Witnesses were mystified as to what they had observed dropping from the sky. Another man and his family passing through the area from the western part of the country also saw the falling object. That man, who was an FAA air traffic control specialist with over sixteen years of experience, supplied me with a detailed statement about what he observed.

The family was traveling in the westbound lane of Route 119 when a double-row cluster of from eight to twelve bright, emerald-green lights suddenly appeared in the sky about two miles away above a hill. The lights were rapidly dropping in the sky, and in a few seconds the object disappeared below the hills. No shape could be determined in the dark. As their car approached the area where the object had been observed, he saw two men putting out a fire. The man stopped to assist in extinguishing the fire. In speaking with the two men, he learned that they had also seen the object, which they were able to determine had a round shape.

The controller indicated that the object's lighting pattern would have made it larger than a B747 or C5A aircraft. He also stated, "The object seen had definite characteristics of a flying controlled object. No high-voltage arcing from the power lines or multiple fireworks flares or rockets could have produced the visual presentation of this sighting."

The witness and others searched the area, but again no sign of an airplane crash could be found. The controller contacted a local fire company and later met some of the firemen at the scene. They discovered a small burned object at the scene. When I learned that this case involved possible physical evidence, we quickly responded to the scene.

When George Lutz and I arrived, we took photographs and measurements. We also obtained samples to analyze from the burned areas, and took radiation readings. With more people calling the UFO Hotline, we learned additional details about the UFO sighting that evening. It seemed that this object was observed in about a ten-mile area. It was first observed coming from the direction of Uniontown by residents in Connellsville in Fayette County.

The object moved along the Youghiogheny River at Connellsville and traveled in a wobbling manner, only about one hundred feet above the ground. Some witnesses, depending on their position, only saw the odd light formation, while others were able to observe a solid-structured object. Two witnesses from Connellsville were sitting on a sundeck as they saw the object approaching along the river. The object appeared to be solid and round in shape, and surrounded in yellow lights. The object continued to move in the direction of New Stanton.

Two passengers in a car exiting from Mount Pleasant onto Route 119 were startled as a large elongated object with bright lights on it moved from left to right over their car about one hundred fifty feet above them. The object was estimated to be about seventy feet long and made no sound. It first moved west, then circled back eastward where it was seen by many people near the Volkswagen plant.

In that area the object began to descend and gave some people the impression that it was about to crash. Other witnesses were walking on the Hunker side of Old Route 119, which was on the other side of the hill from the fire scene.

From their location they observed the large object descending from the sky and appearing to land somewhere near the VW plant. From their perspective these people were able to see a solid round object with a domed top. Their estimation of size was about fifty feet in diameter. It was covered with numerous yellowish-green lights that remained steady and were larger than standard aircraft navigational lights. The object was last seen moving back toward the direction of Uniontown.

It may just be a coincidence that the fire seemed to appear at the same time that the unknown object passed over. Nothing definitively links the two events. The radiation levels at the scene were all normal. Samples obtained from the burned areas were analyzed and determined to be remnants of a magnesium flare. We are unsure how this relates to the incident. It is quite possible that one of the motorists who stopped to assist may have carried a safety flare with him to the scene. Something strange was seen by many independent witnesses that Labor Day weekend in 1986. That object in the sky still remains unexplained.

UFO over Car Frightens Family
September 7, 1986
Between Connellsville and Vanderbilt

At 9:40 p.m. on September 7, 1986, a woman and her two daughters were traveling on Route 201 between Connellsville and Vanderbilt. They observed an object over a field to their left that they described as a bright white mass of light that contained two separate balls of light within it. As the mass rose into the air, sparks began to fall from it.

The illuminated mass approached the car at a rather low altitude from a distance of about one hundred feet. The object then passed over the front of the car and moved to the right side of the car. Just a little farther down the road, it changed course and moved from left to right. The luminous anomaly then moved over a distant hill and out of their view. Interestingly, considerable static was noted on the FM radio during this event. The sighting lasted about three minutes. The mother told me that she had never believed in such reports, and that she was frightened when the object was above them.

Mysterious Siege in Clearfield County
November 1988
Clearfield County

For several weeks in November 1988, numerous UFO sightings and other strange events happened in Clearfield County, then suddenly stopped. A few of these reports are written below.

At 10:20 p.m. on November 18, 1988, a man driving to work noticed a brilliant light moving through the sky in the area of Graham Township. After he traveled a short distance down the road, he found a better vantage point and had a better view of the object in the sky. From that location he could see a rounded object about sixty feet in diameter and ten feet high hovering just above the trees. The top was flat, and across the front were five or six large square windows from which a bright yellow light was emitted. The light from the object was so bright that it illuminated the surrounding trees and sky. Later several other witnesses reiterated this report, having seen brightly illuminated round objects moving quickly through the sky.

On November 25, 1988, at 6:55 p.m., sections of eastern and western Pennsylvania were among those affected by a major earthquake, the effects of which were measured in other states as well as in Canada. At almost exactly the same moment, five people watching deer near the village of Goshen in Clearfield County saw a large yellow-orange sphere of light suddenly illuminate the sky, then move off and vanish. That area reportedly did not feel any effects of the quake.

Yet another event occurred several hours later. At 1:50 a.m. on November 26, the Clearfield County fire and police departments began to receive numerous reports of a mysterious explosion that shook homes throughout the county. Emergency personnel reportedly searched the area for the source, but nothing was located. Just as the explosion occurred, two police officers from two different departments observed a bright white light move quickly across the sky into the clouds. Both the apparent detonation and the mysterious light seem to have been isolated within that county.

A bolide fireball meteor is an extraordinarily bright meteor that can at times produce a sonic boom. However, it is normally reported over a large geographical area, which does not seem to be the case in this instance.

Two Objects and a Commercial Jet
November 1986
Hopwood

In Hopwood in Fayette County on November 14, 1986, at 5:10 p.m., witnesses saw a large, silver, cylindrical-shaped object hovering for a period of about five minutes. After it began to move slowly, a bright white light appeared on it. A commercial jet then flew into the vicinity. The person reported that the two shapes were easily discernable. The object suddenly sped away with a burst of speed and was out of sight within a few seconds.

A few minutes after the first object left, a second strange object appeared in the same part of the sky where the first object originally was. The second object was charcoal black in color and shaped like a cross. From a height estimated to be a few thousand feet in the air, the object slowly descended downward, then suddenly moved at a fast pace toward Uniontown, and was out of sight again in seconds. Total observation time was about seven minutes. No sound was heard with either sighting.

Chapter 10
Close-Range Observations

Basketball-Sized Sphere Taps on Window
December 31, 1984
Level Green

UFOs have been reported in various shapes and sizes. Here is an account of a small unknown object observed at close range. Early on the evening of December 31, 1984, a man was relaxing and watching television with his sister, who was visiting him. Then two loud taps at the living-room window drew their attention, the drapes being open.

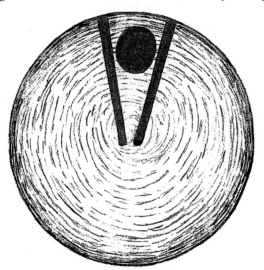

Sketch of small sphere near window.
Stan Gordon Archives

Moments after hearing the taps, a bright red, non-illuminated, basketball-sized spherical object moved slowly toward the right side directly in front of the window. Sitting only six feet from the window, the man saw the object and immediately got up and ran to investigate. He watched as the round object turned sideways then rose upward, noting that the sphere had two beams of light and was giving off some sparks. The object was heading toward the top of a neighbor's house as though it was going to move over the roof. The witness could not see that high from his position. It also moved close to the electric supply line between the two houses.

The man then turned on the outside light and went outside to look around, but he could no longer see the sphere. He returned inside to discuss what had happened with his sister. Just seconds later two more taps were again heard against the window. This time both the man and his sister saw the mystifying sphere. They watched as it moved quite slowly in front of the window, then moved upward again. This time the man turned on all of the outside lights and went outside again and walked around the house, but the object was gone.

After I received the report, I went to the location where the incident occurred, searched for evidence, and gathered all of the details. The object was a little larger than a basketball in size. On the object appeared to be two dark lines that seemed to be black or dark blue in color. These lines extended from the center of the spherical device in a V-like pattern to the top edge. Positioned in the center of the V was a dark round dot, which was the same color as the two lines. The dot gave the witness the impression of an "eye" and was about one inch in diameter.

When the object turned, before it rose the first time, the man noticed that the back section of the sphere was also red in color. He did note another interesting detail. Two beams of brilliant white light, each about sixteen inches long and approximately one inch thick, projected out from the round object.

The beams appeared to extend from the rear-side center of the sphere. The illumination from the beams did not seem to cast any reflective light on the surrounding area. From around both beams a sparking effect was emitted. These people were unaware that I had been receiving other UFO reports from around that same general area for quite some time.

Independent Verification

In many instances over the years, UFO reports were called in to my UFO Hotline number by people unknown to each other, sometimes within minutes, and often from the same general area. They independently described a similar observation that verified the other eyewitness accounts.

Man Stands Underneath UFO
June 21, 1985
Indianhead

Many UFO accounts are on record in which observers report strange objects high in the sky or even just hundreds of feet away. But how often do you hear reports where a witness is close enough to stand directly under an unknown craft? That's exactly what was reported to have happened during the early morning of June 21, 1985.

The witness in this case was shaken up enough by his experience that he called the state police barracks in Uniontown to report what had occurred. He was then given my UFO Hotline number.

It was at about 12:30 a.m. that he was driving his vehicle and passing over a knoll about two miles west of Indianhead in Fayette County when he noticed an odd series of six lights in the sky that he surmised were bright stars.

As he moved closer to the light source, he could see that the lights were connected to an object that he at first thought was the Goodyear blimp. Driving farther down the road, he attempted to flag down another car to point out the craft, but the vehicle refused to slow down. The object appeared to move quite slowly and crossed the road to the right. It appeared solid and was shaped like an elongated blimp, having a solid metallic-silver surface color. He estimated its length to be about one hundred feet.

Curiosity got the best of him and he pulled off to the side of the road, opened the door, and stood there staring at the object. The object itself made no noise while hovering. However, when it moved, he heard a sound "like something enormous moving through the air," describing it as sounding like a "whoosh." The object then moved above the trees to a height of about thirty feet.

Bright blue lights suddenly began to be emitted from the bottom of the object. Interestingly, the lights were bright enough that he could see that the bottom center of the object was hollow. Additionally, six blue lights in the top of the object were described as flashes of high-intensity blue. These lights spun in a counterclockwise pattern and illuminated the trees and the ground surface. The witness soon realized that the object was not a blimp, as it had no gondola.

Artist depiction of UFO hovering over field.
Drawing by Charles Hanna

His attention was drawn to dogs barking at a nearby mobile home, and he ran to let them know of the flying object and to see if he could borrow a camera. Unfortunately, they did not have one. He then ran over to the field where the object was now either hovering or crossing over slowly, being quite low to the ground. The witness stood below it looking all over its surface for markings or symbols, such as a USA emblem, but there was nothing there. He yelled out loudly at the object, but there was no response. The fellow ran back to his vehicle and hurried to his home several miles away where he awakened his parents and told them what had happened. They all returned to the location, but the object had departed the area.

Unknown to this man, a number of other observers had reported similar UFO sightings within hours of each other. At about 11:55 p.m. on June 20, a call came in that several people near Bethel Park, a suburb of Pittsburgh, had seen a huge elliptical-shaped object with many blue and white lights moving slowly overhead.

Then minutes later another report came in from the Castle Shannon area outside of Pittsburgh where a woman said that she watched a three-hundred-foot-long solid oval-shaped object with many lights move about fifty feet over an apartment complex. The object made a low whirring sound as it moved slowly eastward.

Just minutes after midnight on June 21, two men reported a UFO encounter from Jefferson County, which is about ninety miles north of Pittsburgh. They said that they had seen a large, glowing white object with six steady blue lights moving silently about one hundred feet above the ground. Something strange indeed was seen that night by different people over a widespread area.

Movement of UFOs

Not only can the physical appearance of UFOs be quite varied, but the movements of these unknown devices can have unusual patterns as well. Some close-range UFO observers have described the objects hovering, spinning, zigzagging, reversing directions, and in the next case, making a rapid darting motion.

Darting Sphere
September 2, 1989
Ebensburg

A gentleman was sitting by his pond on his rural property at about 3:00 p.m. on a beautiful sunny day on September 2, 1989. A strange object approached from the north and began to hover about thirty feet above the ground over a field where the grass stood about four feet high and which was no more than fifty feet away and from the witness.

The object was described as spherical and about fifteen to twenty feet in diameter. The top section appeared a silver color, while the bottom was colored orange-red. The center was divided by a glasslike, amber-colored window with one green flashing light. The object first hovered for about forty-five seconds, then rose and ascended into the sky. It soon returned to the same spot, where it hovered again for about one and one half minutes before departing from sight.

The object was silent as it moved in rapid jerking movements like those of a hummingbird. Before its final departure from the area, the object emitted a mist from its bottom right side downward toward the ground. After the object had finally departed, the witness found a twelve-foot swirl pattern in the grass beneath the area where the object had been hovering.

Close Encounter in a Cemetery
March 9, 1992
New Kensington

This incident involved two young fellows who gave a detailed account about a UFO they saw at close range. I was notified by the local police about the encounter and an investigation took place soon after.

On the evening of March 9, 1992, two young boys, eight and ten years of age, had an unforgettable experience. The event reportedly occurred about a mile from the Alcoa Research Center near New Kensington. The boys were playing near a cemetery about 6:30 p.m. when they noticed an object in the sky approaching from the east. It gave them the impression of a flying car with two lights.

It flew with a fluttering motion that allowed them to see both the top and bottom sections of the object, as it appeared to be banking back and forth. The object was disc-shaped and of a gray or silver color, with two protrusions from the top. When the object reached about the center of the cemetery, the two headlight-type lights turned off and a bright beam of light was emitted from the bottom center of the object.

At the same time, a large number of round white lights turned on, these being located along the perimeter of the object on both the upper and lower surfaces. The light beam was so intense that it hurt the boys' eyes to look at it. They estimated the size of the object to be about the size of a truck and described its sound as that of a jet engine.

The boys stated that they became frightened and hid behind a tombstone when the object hovered overhead and the beam of light illuminated them. Both boys ran from cover toward the road, which was about one hundred yards away. When the younger boy reached the road, he ran in a circle and realized that the object was following his movements. After this the object turned and proceeded back toward the cemetery. Other low-level UFO sightings were also reported in this general area during this time period.

A Very Close Encounter with a Mini-UFO
July 24, 2002
North Huntingdon

When some folks decided to go to their local shopping center to make a few purchases, the last thing on their mind was seeing something strange and unusual. That is what happened, however, to a small group of people on July 24, 2002. This encounter with a strange flying device occurred in, of all places, the parking lot of a shopping complex off of Route 30, in North Huntingdon Township.

It was around 10:00 p.m. and the stores in the shopping center had closed down for the day. In the parking lot a man and his wife spotted a friend whom they hadn't seen for quite awhile. The three people stood there for some time and got involved in an extended conversation. As the discussion continued, the friend suddenly yelled out, "Look behind you!" The man and his wife turned and looked in that direction. When they turned, they were quite startled to see a small sphere, which was "absolutely round and shiny." The round object, while looking somewhat similar to a bubble, appeared to be a solid device. The witness I interviewed stated, "It was solid, in a way, not like a bubble. You could see thickness in the wall of the object." The sphere seemed to be about the diameter of a tennis ball.

The trio watched as the object moved past them, floating at a distance of less than ten feet away. The man I spoke with told me that, if he would have moved forward just a few feet, he could have reached out and grabbed the unidentified sphere. This witness was not about to do that. As they watched, the mini-sphere moved rather slowly on a straight path down the middle of the roadway. The witness commented that it was on a course, "moving straight as an arrow."

The small globe was moving about six feet above the ground and remained at that level as it continued to move down the road. Then the object made a zigzagging motion toward the left, then toward the right. The object had moved to about halfway down the shopping center when it moved out of view. The object, which made no detectable sound, appeared to have been powered and controlled.

The National Weather Service office in Pittsburgh verified that the winds in the area that night were calm. A witness told me, "It was a very calm night, with no wind at all, yet this bubble zoomed on past us as if being driven by something unseen." As they watched, they saw the object float under an awning of a building. From this it was apparent to the observers that no strings were attached to it. The object also appeared to reflect light from the overhead lighting.

The small sphere was observed for about twenty seconds. No other people were present at the location at the time. The witness who had contacted me about the sighting had previous military experience. He felt that, whatever the object was that he saw, it gave him the impression that "it was a probe of some kind."

UFO Emits Beam toward Aircraft
April 21, 1999
West Mifflin

I received a report from a witness a couple of days after this UFO incident took place. It was about 9:15 p.m. on April 21, 1999, when several people driving near West Mifflin observed something in the sky that they had never seen before. They were familiar with the aircraft following the flight path from the Allegheny County Airport and were surprised to see a nearly triangular-shaped object in the sky.

According to one of the observers, "It looked like an eighth slice of pizza flying with the crust end forward." That forward section of the strange flying object was covered with many non-blinking lights that were all white in color. They could easily see the shape of the object because it was silhouetted against the sky. At the same time that the UFO was observed, they saw what they believed to be a commercial aircraft flying toward Pittsburgh. The triangular object was above the aircraft, and it appeared to suddenly stop as the aircraft moved on.

Moments later the triangular craft began to follow the aircraft, quickly catching up with it.

According to a witness, as the object was positioned diagonally with the airplane, a bright beam of light was suddenly emitted from the side of the triangular object and was directed onto the aircraft. The beam of light initially appeared narrow, then expanded in width, and reportedly completely illuminated the commercial aircraft. Then seconds later the beam suddenly disappeared. The witnesses pulled off the road at that point and ran inside a home to get another person to come out to witness what they were seeing, but when they returned, they could only see a bright light moving across the sky in the distance.

Section 2
Creature Encounters

We have all heard accounts of mysterious creatures that roam forests and lakes throughout the world, across the United States, and even right in our own backyard, here in Pennsylvania. Many of us are familiar with their names: Bigfoot, Yeti, Nessie, Champ, and Mothman. To some people they are just names, thought to be associated with fictionalized creatures that couldn't possibly exist. But what if some mysterious unknown creatures really are out there somewhere? Sightings of Bigfoot, those generally large, hair-covered, manlike or sometimes more apelike creatures, continue to be reported yearly from many locations worldwide, including Pennsylvania.

Numerous other mysterious beasts have been reported for many years from across the Keystone State. Continually reported are sightings of cougars, also known as the mountain lion or panther. Not only have there been well-documented sightings, but also videos have been taken, and casts have been made of paw prints. I made a good cast of such a print in July 1984 in Armstrong County. At that time, police officials called on my PASU research group to investigate a series of up-close mountain lion sightings in the area.

The mystery about these big cats is that they have been declared extinct in Pennsylvania since the late 1800s. No doubt some sightings of these animals can be attributed to exotic pets that have gotten out of control and/or illegally released into the woods and forests of the state. But over the years people have reported seeing more than one adult cougar together at the same time. I have also heard accounts of an adult animal being seeing with cubs. Is it possible that some of the native species of mountain lion have been able to survive in the forests of Pennsylvania?

Much stranger are the accounts of black panthers that have continued to be reported from many locations across the country and here in the Keystone State. These reports are quite interesting since some observations of such animals have been quite detailed, even though this species is not indigenous to this part of the world. Reports of African lions roaming fields across the state have even been filed. In the incidents that I am familiar with, I am not aware of any such animals being captured, or of any reports of escaped wild animals.

We have to look skyward for other mysterious creatures that have been reported not only from the northern tier of the state, but also from many other statewide locations, and from other states as well. Many sightings have been reported of giant birds with massive wingspans up to twenty feet or more in length. These giant flying creatures have become commonly known as "Thunderbirds."

I have interviewed quite a number of people who claim to have seen these huge flying beasts, and some were at quite close range. Additionally, many different really strange creatures have occasionally been reported from time to time. Alleged sightings have been filed on a huge snake-like creature supposedly seen in one of the rivers in Pittsburgh. Other reports have come in of beasts that should not be on the loose but have been occasionally spotted by mystified observers. From African lions to monkeys, out-of-place animals have shown up in the woods of Pennsylvania. Many other strange beings have been reported as well, which some observers felt were related to the presence of strange lights or UFOs in the area.

Chapter 11
Witness/Creature Interaction

UFOs and Bigfoot
September 13, 1983
Connellsville

On September 13, 1983, I received a phone call on my UFO Hotline from a man who lived near Connellsville in Fayette County. The man and some neighbors were watching two strange star-like objects in the sky that were changing colors from red to white. While under observation, one of the objects moved across the sky, dropped downward, and then hovered. Then the object suddenly shot across the sky toward the west and moved out of sight within seconds.

The man who called me about the strange lights in the sky revealed some other events that had taken place in the same area for the past few months, but seemed to be escalating during the last couple of days. He explained how his young child was awakened during the night and was screaming, shaking, and staring at the window facing a garden. He had also noticed that his pets had been disturbed and frightened during this time period. What had really alarmed the man was when he discovered the vegetables in his garden knocked down and a large footprint in the garden about ten feet from the window of the room where his child slept. The family had also been hearing strange baby-crying sounds that seemed to cause a reaction from the local wildlife. Once the cries were heard, the surroundings became silent and the pets and young child suddenly became frightened.

The next day I led a PASU team to Fayette County to investigate this recent sighting of strange lights in the sky, and other events. We interviewed the man who initially reported the incident and others who were involved. After this, the initial witness reluctantly revealed details of a close encounter that he had with a Bigfoot creature in August of 1982 while fishing at a pond outside of Connellsville. The man had been fearful to talk about what he had seen with those close to him, thinking that they would consider him crazy. The witness, though, was certain of what he had seen.

On the day of the incident, the man was sitting on a log near the edge of the water. It was early evening, and the fisherman had been there only a short time when he heard some movement behind him in the woods. He didn't pay much attention to the sounds, assuming that another person was in the area. Just a short time later the fellow turned and was so frightened by what he saw that he fell backward off the log.

About forty-five yards away stood a huge, hair-covered, manlike creature that he estimated was almost eight feet tall. The creature stood upright and was motionless as it stared toward the fisherman. The creature was covered with dark hair, yet the hair around the head area was a smoky gray color. The facial hair appeared to be lighter than other areas of the body. The creature's eyes were described as large, dark, and deep set. The arms were long, hanging down past the knees, and the hands appeared larger than that of a human.

The feet appeared to be large and covered with hair. As he continued to watch the creature, he detected a musty smell in the air. The staring match between the man and the beast continued for what seemed to be several minutes. He was uncertain if he should stay where he was or run away. Suddenly the creature turned and reached out its arms, parting some tree branches as it walked into the woods ahead.

The witness was reluctant to tell us what had also occurred during the face-to-face confrontation with the unknown hairy beast. The man said that, in his mind, he was thinking while looking at the creature, "What are you?" The man stated that although he was somewhat frightened of the animal, he wanted it to come closer and try to communicate with it. He said a strange inner warmth came over him, and he felt a heavy pressure move across his forehead. The man said that he had a feeling that the creature was trying to impress a message into his mind, but he could not perceive the information. It was difficult for the witness to relate this to us.

Footprint found near pond.
Copyright Stan Gordon

Another person living near this area told us that something had been pounding on her mobile home. She had also heard strange baby-crying sounds.

The man frequently fished at the same pond where he had the creature encounter in 1982. We went to the pond while in the area to look around, since this witness stated that, just a few days before, he had seen several large footprints around the fishing area that went into the woods.

While looking over the terrain, we located one large, three-toed footprint that was similar to other tracks that had been found in other state locations in past years. The track had water seeping into it and could not be cast, so only photos were taken.

While rarely reported, I have investigated and written about other incidents where both a UFO and Bigfoot creature have been seen together simultaneously. In some other cases UFOs have been reported in a local area, then reports of large footprints or other possible Bigfoot activity soon followed. What, if any, direct connection exists between the two anomalies is still open for speculation.

Hiker Stares Down Bigfoot
December 1986
Gray Station

This event involves a man who was walking near Gray Station in early December of 1986. It was about dusk as the man walked on the pathway that led out of the woods near the railroad tracks, when suddenly a large tree branch was thrown at his feet. He looked up to see a creature farther down the path, standing motionless and just staring at him.

He described the creature as standing about eight to nine feet tall with a large head, broad shoulders, its arms hanging down below its knees, and covered with hair. The eyes of the creature were widely separated, and the fingers appeared unusually long. The fellow said he could hear the animal making a heavy breathing noise. For five long minutes they had a visual standoff. Then the creature suddenly turned and took a large step over a bank, moving out of the man's line of sight. As the creature ran off, it did so in a stooped fashion. The ground was frozen at the time and the man said he could hear heavy footsteps as the creature moved off.

Location where hiker confronted creature.
Copyright Stan Gordon

This fellow, who had spent many years in the woods, was now reluctant to walk in that area as a direct result of this encounter. He told me that he was hesitant to pursue the creature, as he was stunned by the encounter, or possibly evenly slightly in shock.

Cub Scout Spots Bigfoot
Week of February 14, 1988
Ligonier

During February and March of 1988, PASU was busy investigating several alleged sightings of the Bigfoot creature. Two of these reports came from two different locations along the Chestnut Ridge in Westmoreland County. One such incident involved an eight-year-old cub scout. I interviewed the youngster in person and he gave me his account of seeing "an ape" in the woods.

The young scout and his family lived on the Ligonier side of Chestnut Ridge. During the week of February 14, 1988, he was playing in a wooded area near his home when he noticed ahead of him a tall humanlike figure, but it was covered with dark brown hair. The creature was about one hundred fifty feet away and was just standing there when it apparently realized that it was being observed.

It turned and looked at the boy for about a minute, then walked deeper into the woods. The youth said its arms hung down below its knees, and he noticed a strong smell in the air "like a wet dog, but much stronger." The boy waited for a while, but the creature did not return. He was curious as to what it was, since he could only describe it as "a big ape walking like a man." He walked over to the spot where it had been standing, and it was there he found a number of footprints in the muddy area, all of which were about fifteen inches long and had indistinct toes, possibly four in number.

When he told his parents about his experience, they told him that it was just his imagination. But the boy was insistent that he had seen the creature. He went to the library to locate some books on wildlife of the world to try to find the animal he had seen. Except for a gorilla, nothing in the books was even close to its appearance.

Bigfoot Visits a Baseball Field
July 30, 1982
Youngwood-New Stanton

During the summer of 1982, I was contacted about an encounter with a tall, hair-covered creature that fit the description of "Bigfoot." I went to the location where the sighting had occurred, spoke with witnesses, and searched for evidence. I learned that, on the evening of July 30, 1982, two couples decided to take a moonlit walk to a scenic lookout located between Youngwood and New Stanton.

It was about 11:00 p.m. when they decided to walk down a local road. As they started moving up to the top of a hill, they began to hear a rattling and hissing noise coming from above them. When they reached the top, they noticed something odd in the distance. In the area where the sounds were coming from sat a capped gas well, which was moving back and forth as though someone was shaking it. This activity soon ceased. The group of people continued to walk toward the opposite side of the hill that overlooks the area.

The couples sat there for a while enjoying the evening when one of the men heard a low moaning and whining noise in the distance, and mentioned it to the others. The others heard nothing and kept on talking. A short time later the same man and one of the women both heard the sounds at the same time.

The noise began to increase in volume, and soon all four people heard it. Initially the sounds were somewhat frightening, but after a period of time, the group of people began to relax, laughed, and even loudly mocked the sounds. As the people continued their vocalizations, the strange sounds got even louder and the source seemed to be moving closer to their location.

One fellow was concerned that the moaning sound might be coming from someone who was hurt and, much to his wife's distress, stated that he was going to have a look. She pleaded with him not to go. It was about then that the moaning sounds began to fade again and the couple began to relax and joked about what had happened.

Then out of the silence they heard a rustling sound coming from their left, near a baseball field. One man noticed that, about twenty five yards away, something large and dark in color appeared to be moving close to the ground. The group got up and looked in that direction. One of the men noticed that his friend's eyes were very large as he stared intently at something. That's when he saw it.

Something huge, about seven to nine feet tall, was standing upright beside the baseball backstop. One fellow yelled for everyone to get out of there. His friend, though, stood for a couple of minutes observing the strange creature that appeared to be motionless at that point, while the rest of the group slowly backed away. But when it began to move quickly toward the group with long strides and long arms swinging, fear overtook them and they ran toward the road that led down the hillside. One woman began screaming and had to be pulled along by her husband to leave the area.

After quickly reaching the bottom of the hill, they looked back and saw the lofty creature moving toward the hillside as though it were going to come down the hill after them. They continued home and called the police. The police did go to the location but nothing was found.

The description of what they saw was that of a huge, hair-covered, manlike creature that stood between seven to nine feet tall and was estimated to have weighed between three hundred fifty to four hundred fifty pounds. Dark fur covered its large, muscular upper body, and legs. Its arms were long, and its hands hung down below the knees.

The creature at times appeared stooped and stood with its legs slightly bent. When it walked, it moved in a forward arm-swinging motion with an unusual gait. With each step the right arm and right leg moved forward, and then the left arm and left leg moved forward.

The witnesses had no doubt that they saw a creature that was quite strange and unknown to them, and they knew it was not a bear.

Chapter 12
Traces

Footprints and the Electric Fence
October 30, 1986
Unity Township

A resident from a rural area in Unity Township, not far from Latrobe, called me on October 30, 1986. While taking a walk that morning, he came across a number of large, strange footprints. I quickly went out to that location to interview the witness and to look over the area. Upon arrival I learned that, since that past summer, the electric fence on the property had been broken on five occasions. The family had purchased some horses and had erected the fence line around a few acres.

The fence had been broken at different locations. The top of the three-wire fence was about four feet high. At times the top strand was broken, yet other times it would be broken around the bottom. The man thought there was the possibility that somehow a horse was doing this, but after our findings on that day, he felt that something else was involved.

In this instance, at the top of a high hill, the four-foot-high top wire on the fence was found broken alongside a crushed electric insulator. Alongside of this were three quite strange footprints on the ground. The number of toes were not clearly defined, but they looked similar to the famous cast of a three-toed footprint that I had taken outside of Greensburg on August 7, 1973. That footprint was thirteen inches long and eight inches wide. The fact that this footprint measured exactly the same as the one I had cast thirteen years before was of great interest to me. I made a cast of the best track, since the ground conditions were not good for casting.

About two months earlier a neighbor had been taking a walk up this particular hill when they heard an unusual sound, like that of an animal wheezing. Additionally, they also heard the sound of something heavy moving off through the woods. During this same time period a rabbit was found with its neck broken. Also two cats were found in an unusual manner: one with its intestines hanging out and the other with a broken neck. A woman who lived just down the road reportedly called the state police when she heard a loud strange sound, similar to a woman screaming in pain. This area is located in the general region that has had a lot of Bigfoot activity reported over the years.

What Left Strange Footprints in Mercer County?
March 13, 1989
Wheatland

On March 13, 1989, near Wheatland in Mercer County, a woman reported an unusual incident. About 7:15 p.m., the dog started to run back and forth in the house and then began to growl. The dog wanted to go outside, so the woman let him out, but he soon returned inside. The dog started going back and forth to the doors and wanted out again. The woman thought that the dog smelled something outside.

Concerned that something was wrong, she called out to her husband. He took their pet outside, and the dog began to track something through the yard to the edge of the woods. After about five minutes the dog began to pursue whatever was moving ahead of them. The man could hear the sounds of something heavy running through the woods, along with the apparent sound of tree branches snapping as it made its way ahead.

The man called to his dog to come back, then returned to the house, perplexed by what was in the woods. Meanwhile his wife had also heard the noises from the woods. Soon after, they took the dog outside and it led them to a number of footprints close to the side of their home. The positioning of the tracks suggested that the creature had turned at one point and moved in the direction of the woods. The five-toed footprints measured about eleven inches long and five and one half inches wide. The stride was estimated to be approximately four feet from heel to toe.

The family was shaken up enough by the incident to call the local police, who came to the house to investigate. The police officer found a wide path that had been knocked down by something that had moved through that area. They also called the Pennsylvania Game Commission and another agency, but neither was able to identify the tracks. I met with the man and his wife and interviewed them about their experience.

Fresh Footprints in the Snow
February 1996
South Connellsville

It was late evening in February 1996 when a sound was heard outside a witness's home. Looking outside, the witness observed a series of footprints in the freshly falling snow. Upon examination the footprints were estimated to be about fifteen inches in length, with a large stride between the tracks. The tracks continued for a distance. At one point whatever made the tracks stepped over a woodpile and continue over a bank.

The witness was intrigued enough to take several photographs of the impressions. Having lived in that area for many years, she had never seen such unusual footprints before. This location is in the heart of the Chestnut Ridge, an area which has historically produced many reported encounters with Bigfoot.

Chapter 13
Government Interaction?

The FBI and the Derry Township Creature
March 12, 1997
Derry Township

A profoundly strange event occurred in a rural location of Westmoreland County in Derry Township. It was during the early morning hours of March 12, 1997, when I answered a call on my UFO/Bigfoot Hotline. The voice on the phone seemed a little nervous, and the caller began to relate the details of what had occurred at about 3:00 a.m., involving himself and two friends.

These young men worked during the night and were driving down a rural road when a hubcap came off their vehicle and rolled across the road into a field in the vicinity of some old cars. A short time later they returned to that area to try to recover the missing hubcap. Their vehicle was parked about two hundred fifty feet from the field. One fellow remained inside the car. The other two men began to search for the wheel cover. After a short time the silence was suddenly broken by an odd sound described as being "like metal on metal," and then by what seemed to be a growl from a dog. They moved slowly away from that spot. The one fellow yelled to his companion to stop as he saw something moving ahead. Fear engulfed the two men when one of them shined a flashlight on the source of the noise.

What they saw was not a dog, but a huge, white-hair-covered, ape-like creature rising up from the ground. A feeling of panic came over one fellow as the creature stared at the two men. That man quickly ran off toward the parked vehicle and yelled to the driver in the vehicle to start the motor. The other man continued to stare at the creature for what seemed like unending moments, then quickly ran off as well.

As the trio pulled away, one of the fellows told his friends that he had dropped his father's expensive knife, and some keys as well. As they passed near the location where they had seen the creature, the lost items were not seen, so they pulled over to see if they could spot them. They were not located, and they left the area.

Then another odd event occurred. As they left the scene and drove just a short distance, an upscale red and silver Chevy dual-wheel truck passed them in the opposite direction at a fast pace. The trio watched as this truck pulled onto a side road, then turned around and began to follow them down the road. The Chevy truck increased its speed and came right up to the rear bumper of their vehicle, keeping that position for about half a mile. Each man in the car had the feeling that whoever was in the truck was obtaining their license number.

Finally, the truck stopped abruptly in the roadway, started backing up, turned its lights off, and backed onto a side road. The three witnesses continued on to one of their residences. When discussing the events, two of them decided to go back to the location where they saw the creature in order to find the knife and keys, as well to see if they could spot the creature again and determine what it was. The third man had no interest in returning to look around, so he stayed at the residence.

One of the men was very proud of his car, which he had put a lot of work into and which was equipped with a modified high-speed engine. The two men drove that car back to the field area. The men also took with them an automobile headlight that they had converted to use as a high-powered spotlight.

When they arrived, they shined the spotlight around the field and the old vehicles, and a short time later the creature appeared again. The beam of light was directed on the creature. This time the two men got a good look at the mysterious beast. The blinding light was concentrated on its head area, and the beast appeared to be getting agitated by the concentrated bright beam. Walking upright on two legs, it began to chase the car and got to within about three feet from the rear bumper. It continued to follow them for a short distance as they pulled away from it and left the area.

Chapter 13 Government Interaction?

The creature was observed in several different positions during the various events, such as first stooped, then later on all fours, and also walking upright like a human. The sound of something heavy was apparent when the creature moved across the ground.

The men described the creature as standing at least nine feet tall, apelike in appearance, and covered with long white hair, about eight to ten inches long. Another outstanding physical feature was the length of its arms, which were so long that they hung down to the knees or just below them. The creature was quite muscular and broad shouldered. The observers did notice that the eyes, which seemed pinkish in color, appeared almost egg shaped. The creature did not seem to have any neck.

The final encounter with the creature that night was most dramatic. The owner of the modified-engine car decided to make one last attempt on his own to find the knife and keys he had dropped in the field. He returned alone and drove slowly past the area. Not seeing the strange creature, he pulled into the field and soon spotted the knife. He never got out of his car, but opened the door, reached out, and grabbed the knife. He kept driving around the area quite slowly trying to locate the keys. Then suddenly he felt a heavy thump toward the rear of his car.

The driver looked into his rear mirror and was shocked to see the huge, hairy creature leaning on the back of the car, peering at him through his rear window. Its eyes seemed to have a reddish glow. The driver pushed down hard on the gas, trying to quickly exit the area, but the car wouldn't move.

As the man continued to hit the gas, the sound from his tailpipes was getting louder by the moment. Suddenly the creature was no longer on the car, and he was able to make a quick getaway. The man felt certain that it was the car's high-pitched noise that finally made the creature leave the vehicle alone. The man later found a convenience store open and went inside to get something to eat and de-stress. He parked his car nearby so that he could keep his eye on it. When he returned to his car, he saw several teenagers checking out his car. He became more alarmed after they asked him if he had been attacked by some kind of animal, as there appeared to be claw marks on the back of the vehicle. The man looked, and there in the paint and metal on the rear of the vehicle were two long scratches.

Photo of scratch marks on trunk of car.
Photograph used with permission of the owner.

The day after the incident, the driver went back to the location of the strange encounter during the daylight. The ground was hard from the cold weather and no footprints could be seen where the creature had been. After I spoke with the initial caller about the events that happened earlier that morning, I made contact with the others involved and made arrangements to meet later that day for an interview, and to examine and photograph the damaged car. The second party I talked with by phone was the man who accompanied the driver of the car with the modified engine, and who had shined the spotlight on the creature.

We discussed the events and set up a time to meet. I learned later that other intriguing events had taken place with two of the witnesses shortly after our phone calls. Apparently, about ten minutes after I had spoken with the second party on the phone, he received a disturbing phone call. As best he could remember, the caller said, "This is Field Agent [name protected] from the Federal Bureau of Investigation. About the incidents last night, forget about what you saw, and I strongly suggest that you don't talk any further with Stan Gordon." Then the caller hung up.

The other man received a phone message that reportedly said, "Stay away. Leave it alone. Forget about it." He was also informed by his relatives that some men drove up to his house in Chevy Caprice cars (often used by law enforcement officers at that time). Two men were in each vehicle, and they wanted to talk with the fellow who was driving the car during the previous night's incident. After these occurrences the men were not contacted again.

Whether or not it was actually the FBI that was involved with this incident is unconfirmed. I did write a letter to the Pittsburgh FBI office, but never received a reply. Regardless of who these mysterious people were, how did they learn of this incident, and how did they know that the witnesses had contacted me?

Chapter 14
Close-Range Observations

Unexpected Visitor at a Camp
March 19, 1983
Armstrong County

It was the afternoon on March 19, 1983, when campers were having a great time preparing fires to keep warm and were hiking around the nearby woods. But something reportedly occurred at that campsite in Armstrong County that apparently frightened some of those in attendance.

While a small group of campers was pumping water, a large, hair-covered creature suddenly entered the campground from the surrounding woods. The animal slowly began walking toward the people, who quickly ran away. Witnesses described a hair-covered manlike creature, about six and a half feet tall with broad shoulders, narrow hips, and a peak on the top of its head.

Walking upright, the beast continued to move around the perimeter of the campsite, then returned to the woods. The creature reportedly came to within thirty feet of some of the observers. To protect themselves, some of the campers reportedly bent coat hangers over the door knobs of their cabins in an effort to prevent the creature from entering their dwellings.

The local authorities were called, but a search of the area revealed no concrete evidence of the animal. Later in the evening the campers conducted their own search, as they were still uneasy about their unexpected visitor. What they noticed in the camp area then was an odd chemical odor they described as similar to sulfur. No further sighting reports were received from this camp.

Police Search for Black Panther
March 30, 1983
Pittsburgh

It is generally known that animals described by observers as black panthers do not exist in this part of world. Although they are not supposed to exist in our area, over the years numerous sightings have been reported of large, black wild cats seen here in Pennsylvania and in others areas of the United States. No doubt some of these sightings could be attributed to escaped captive or exotic pets, but some of the accounts seem odd indeed.

One such event occurred in a populated suburb of Pittsburgh on March 30, 1983. More than one observer was involved, but the primary witness was an auto body mechanic at a large car dealership in Bloomfield. As I conducted the detailed interview with the mechanic, it was apparent that he was quite shaken after the sighting and was certain about what he had seen.

Early in the morning at about 9:30, the mechanic was replacing a headlight on a car when he heard a loud thump nearby. Looking up, he saw a huge black cat leap over the fender and hood of a car in the lot. The panther was carrying a dead animal in its mouth, which was believed to be a large dead rat. The animal was described as having a body three and a half feet long with a tail about four feet long.

He described the animal as "just beautiful," with a solid-black, shiny body. It had a large head. The ears were upright, but the man wasn't sure if they were pointed or rounded off. The eyes were dark, and the fanglike teeth were a brownish color. The big cat made a continuous sound, which was described to me as "not a growl and not a meow, but like deep heavy breathing." A putrid smell like a urine odor also emanated from the animal.

The animal quickly made its way back into the woods from where it came. At about the same time, I was told that a group of people, including the mechanic, also saw a second black panther that appeared to be smaller than the first animal in the woods. There was concern that such wild animals loose in the area might harm someone.

Soon after being contacted, the Pittsburgh police arrived and conducted an extensive two-hour search of the area along with some animal control officers. Weapons and tranquilizer guns were carried for protection and possible capture, but the animals were not found. The police reportedly found some tracks in the area, and some traps were set up.

The local Highland Park Zoo was contacted, but they reported no escaped animals. The mechanic, who wasn't the only witness, found himself ridiculed. He was certain, however, that he saw a black panther at close range. It is interesting that this event occurred in this section of Pittsburgh that has been historically called "Panther Hollow." That was an area where, many years ago, tawny-colored mountain lions, also called cougars or panthers, roamed the land.

Bigfoot Steps over Barbwire Fence
September 27, 2002
Derry Township

I received a phone call on September 28, 2002, from a man who lived with his family in a remote rural location in Derry Township. The man wanted to inform me that two separate family members on different occasions had seen a creature he described as a Bigfoot. After receiving permission to interview those involved and to search for evidence, I packed up my gear. My wife, Debbie, accompanied me to the area to assist with photography.

The man's son had the first encounter on September 11, 2002, during the early evening. The young fellow appeared very serious and gave us a detailed account of what had taken place. When riding a bicycle, he heard crashing sounds coming from the woods. It sounded as though something was hitting a log, along with branches being broken.

Photo of author and fence where creature stepped over.
Copyright Stan Gordon

About three hundred feet ahead, he saw "a big, brown, human-looking thing, but very tall." The creature was moving along the tree line, but at times in various clearings, the youngster got a good look at the strange animal. He described it as manlike, covered with dark brown hair, and standing about eight feet tall. The head of the beast was somewhat cone-shaped, and the animal appeared to be broad shouldered and had long arms. The creature appeared to move in a stooped manner, but took very long strides as it walked. The fellow ran home to tell his father what he had seen. They quickly searched the area, but found no signs of their uninvited visitor.

An even more amazing daylight encounter took place during the afternoon of September 27, when the man's wife was driving away from their house. She was talking to her husband on the cell phone as the event unfolded. She heard something that sounded like tree limbs breaking in the woods to her left, and she assumed that a deer was about to exit the forest. She slowed down, expecting to see a deer run from the woods, but instead saw a tall, manlike creature emerge from a clearing in the woods. She quickly told her husband what had happened.

The creature was covered with long brown hair that appeared to be about twelve inches in length. It stood about eight feet tall, and was quite broad shouldered. The arms were long, hanging down to around its knees. She saw the creature in an open field about forty-five yards from her car.

The creature was slightly hunched over as it walked across the open field. With its long strides it covered the one-hundred-foot-long field quickly. Oddly, the creature did not swing its arms as it moved. The witness looked on as the creature reached the edge of the field. The woman watched in amazement as the creature stepped over the barbwire fence without slowing down or breaking stride. The creature continued walking deeper into the woods and was lost from sight. The woman remained on the phone with her husband during the sighting, becoming more frightened as each second passed. That fence, by the way, was forty-four inches high.

During my investigation I was unable to locate any hair or other evidence on the barbwire fence, or any footprints. Both witnesses appeared to be sincere and credible, wanting no publicity. I had been out in that general area many times since the early 1970s, as many local residents had reported encountering similar creatures.

Why People Want Anonymity

People have often been the unfortunate objects of ridicule when they share their experiences of UFOs, Bigfoot, strange creatures, ghosts, and other paranormal events. Many of those I interviewed have asked me not to identify them as the source of information because of their professional positions or just not wanting to be ridiculed. I have kept in touch with many witnesses years after their experience and found that, even after such a long time, their lives were still impacted by their encounter with the unexplained. I have kept a policy of maintaining anonymity to those observers who have requested it.

Hairy Creature Nearly Hit by Car
July 10, 2009
Uniontown

On July 10, 2009, a strange occurrence took place on a two-lane road in Fayette County, outside the city of Uniontown. The location is about fifty miles southeast of Pittsburgh. The report was initially received by the Sasquatch Watch of Virginia, which then referred the sighting to Eric Altman, the Director of the Pennsylvania Bigfoot Society (PBS), to investigate (www.pabigfootsociety.com).

A PBS team comprising Eric Altman and members Dave and Cindy Dragosin went to the scene on July 15, 2009, to look over the area for any evidence and to interview the witness. Eric invited me to take part in the investigation. It was about 6:00 p.m. on a warm and clear day when the encounter occurred. A woman was driving in her car at about thirty-five to forty miles per hour and watching the road ahead. Then suddenly, out of the corner of her eye, she saw to her left what she thought was a person approaching her vehicle, as though someone was about to walk in front of her car. She thought she was going to crash right into him. So, rather than hit the person, she swerved quickly to the right side of the road, thankful that no other cars or pedestrians were there at the time. As she swerved, she looked at the figure again and realized that she was not looking at a human being, but an odd hair-covered creature.

As the woman sat there momentarily, she looked in her rearview mirror and saw that the creature was now behind her car. She watched in amazement as the creature leaped across the trunk area, explaining that she "looked just in time to see it leap." Very shaken, she sat there a few more seconds, trying to sort out in her mind what had just occurred. When she looked up toward her right, the hairy beast was running down a side road about seventy-five feet away, then it moved out of sight.

The episode lasted just several seconds, but the woman had a chance to get a good look at the creature since this was a close-range sighting in daylight conditions. The creature was described as a dark-colored and hair-covered manlike creature. The witness felt that it was "at least six feet tall or slightly taller." The head was described as large and elongated, and covered in hair that looked "wild." It's neck was rather odd looking, as it was hair covered, but it seemed to be thin and long. According to the woman who saw it, "the neck looked strange because the head was so big and the shoulders were wide."

The creature walked upright on two legs and had long arms that hung down to the knees or past the knees. The hair on its arms was described as being quite long, similar to ape hair. The eyewitness thought the hands were also covered with hair. The creature had wide shoulders that were rounded, and it was stocky and muscular in appearance. It's chest was also covered with thick hair. The woman stated that, while she didn't see any muscles, the creature appeared to be in quite good physical shape from the way it moved.

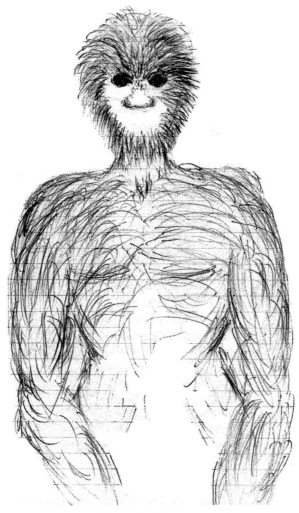

Drawing of creature based on eyewitness accounts.
Drawing used with permission of
the Pennsylvania Bigfoot Society (PBS) and Dave Dragosin (artist)

The woman recalled a detailed description of it's facial features. The face itself was hair covered; however, an exposed area looked white, and a major contrast could be seen in color from the hair. The nose was flat and dark; the ears were hair covered and could not be seen. The mouth area was not clearly seen. Hair protruded from all over the face, similar to that of a canine or a wolf. These features gave the woman the impression that it was older in age.

The witness stated that it was the eyes that really caught her attention and scared her. They were somewhat circular in shape and at least twice as large as that of a human. In describing them, she talked about "the fierceness, the wild look…. It looked like it was crazy." The eyes were dark, possibly black, and were wide set. She said the eyes had "no iris, no whites." She believes that is why the eyes looked so strange. No unusual odors or sounds were detected during the occurrence. The driver did have her windows up, and the air conditioner running at the time.

After the incident the woman drove to a safe area to park and sat there, trying to find an explanation for what she had seen. She tried to rationalize that this was just a human, maybe a person in a costume, but after reviewing what had happened, she ruled out that possibility. The creature was running very fast, directly into the path of her car, and it did not seem to care that it was going to be hit by the car. Also, the speed and agility of the creature, as evidenced when it leaped over the trunk of the car, seemed beyond the ability of a human being.

Inspection of the wooded area revealed no unusual signs or evidence of the creature's presence. We also looked over the car for any evidence as well. When I examined the back of the car, a large scratched area on the left side got my attention. The family had never noticed this scratched area on the car before. Dave and I measured the scratches of the damaged area, which was located about six inches from the left taillight. The affected area was about eight and a half inches long and two inches in width.

Numerous vertical and horizontal thin scratch lines penetrated the paint surface. While it is uncertain, the possibility exists that this damage might have been caused by contact from the creature as it leaped across the trunk of the car. The creature was last seen walking in a direction that would have taken it through a heavily wooded area toward Jumonville. This is another area where I have investigated many other Bigfoot sightings.

Thunderbird Encounters
Pennsylvania and West Virginia

For many years Pennsylvania residents—living primarily in the six counties that make up the Black Forest region of the state—have reported seeing abnormally large birds with huge wingspans estimated to be in the range of twenty feet or more in length. However, many other sightings have come from other sections of the Keystone State, also reporting giant flying creatures where in some cases witnesses claimed the creature looked more like an extinct prehistoric species than anything else. The term "Thunderbird" has been commonly associated with these reported observations.

A number of detailed observations of these alleged flying giants have come to my attention. No doubt in some cases people seeing ordinary birds from various distances and under certain conditions have mistakenly believed that they were seeing a flying creature much larger and more unusual than it really was.

A number of years ago I spoke with a woman, who along with other people, observed a humongous creature flying low over the Westmoreland Mall in Greensburg. This observation occurred during the early morning hours as people waited in line until the next morning to purchase tickets for a music concert. As I recall the report, it was a moonlit night when a huge shadow came over the crowd. They looked up to see a creature with giant wings and a huge beak that looked like a prehistoric bird.

Another witness taking a walk along Route 119 in South Greensburg reported seeing a similar flying monstrosity on September 25, 2001. It was just turning dark when the fellow told me he heard a sound above the moving traffic that sounded "like flags flapping in a thunderstorm."

It was then that he saw a huge dark bird that appeared to be black or dark grayish-brown in color. The creature was flying over trucks and cars about fifty to sixty feet overhead. The bird's head was around three feet long, about the size of a small dog. The fellow was startled by the length of the wingspan, which he felt was between ten to fifteen feet.

The man stated, "I wouldn't say it was flapping its wings gracefully, but almost horrifically flapping its wings very slowly, then gliding above the passing big rig trucks." As the witness watched, the giant bird flew down the road approximately one hundred fifty feet to a wooded area. The bird spread its wings, revealing its massive wingspan as it dropped down to rest on an old tree near a billboard.

Seconds later the bird rose from the tree, which gave the witness the impression that the old tree would break from the weight of the creature. The bird flew out of view toward another wooded area and was not seen again. The man said he had it under unobstructed observation for over a minute.

No other witness came forward to report this particular observation. Soon after, however, I received a call from another man who told me that he had seen a similar giant flying creature in this same area several years before. Also of interest are other reports I received from various individuals—only about a mile away from this location—who reported strange sounds and unusual footprints.

While this book and my investigations have focused on cases from my home state of Pennsylvania, on occasion I receive strange encounter reports from neighboring states as well. One of the most detailed accounts concerning a reported encounter with a possible thunderbird occurred in West Virginia in the fall of 2007.

The witness, whom I interviewed on several occasions, provided a detailed account of what he experienced at about 8:00 a.m. on the morning of the incident. The man was traveling on a two-lane rural road outside of Clendenin, in Kanawha County. The driver had to suddenly hit his brakes hard to avoid hitting a huge bird only a few yards ahead, feeding on road kill.

The man was startled by the size of the creature, which stood at least four feet tall, its head extending above the roof line of his car. The head was dominant, but not overly proportioned to its body. The head was featherless and separated from the rest of the body by a prominent yellowish-orange collar of plumage.

The body was covered with dark brown or black feathers. The neck appeared long and crooked. The beak appeared dark, and was quite large and long. The eyes were dark in color. The witness did not recall much detail about the feet; however, the legs were covered in feathers, but the feet were bare. The chest of the giant fowl was distinct in that it was well formed.

The witness pointed out that the most striking feature was the massive wingspan, which was easily as wide as the two-lane road. The man actually went back to the site and measured the distance of the roadway from edge to edge. It was twenty-one feet across! The witness stated, "The wings were, as I can remember, as arms of a human are attached. It had shoulders. It had a very muscular upper torso, and the wings were as if they were its arms."

The driver went on to say that when he came upon the animal, "We both startled each other it seems, for it looked as shocked as I was." When the bird became startled, it pulled its head back to stare at the driver. The bird then ran from the car as if it were going to fly off in an awkward manner. It ran jumping from one foot to the other in a hopping manner while flapping its wings to gain speed for takeoff. The witness said that it was similar to a jumping-hopping run, and it moved about five yards. Then, with its huge wings, the creature lifted itself off the ground.

The man said the wingtips stirred up dust and gravel on both sides of the road as it ran to become airborne. The bird flew away over the treetops and was not seen after that. The witness began to look at books about birds to try to identify what he had seen. The closest specimen was a drawing of an extinct bird called a teratorn.

Chapter 15
Food Sources?

Berry-Picking Hairy Creature
August 9, 1991
Between Westmoreland and Indiana Counties

On August 9, 1991, a group of young fellows were spotting deer in the woods one evening near the border of Westmoreland and Indiana counties. They soon saw more than they expected in their light beams. About two hundred feet away, they observed a dark, hair-covered creature standing upright and eating berries.

At first they thought it was a bear, but after watching the creature for more than five minutes, they realized that they were seeing an animal much different than a bear. The group also noticed a sulfur smell in the air at the same time of the sighting. The creature had red eyes, and as it reached up for the berries and continued to eat them, the creature always had its eyes toward the group of observers. The creature remained standing the entire time. The fellows became unnerved after their estimated five-minute observation and left the area.

The next day they returned with other people to search the area of the sighting. The foliage was flattened in the area where the creature had stood. The berry plants were picked clean and smashed down. To gauge the height of the creature, one man who was over six feet tall stood at the spot where the creature was sighted while the others returned to their original vantage point. Using this, they estimated that the creature was over nine feet tall.

Bigfoot Chases Deer
March 19, 1988
Derry Township

In the early morning of March 19, 1988, at 12:45 a.m., a man driving on a back road in Derry Township was startled when a deer ran across the road about five car lengths in front of him. That was alarming enough, but the man was even more startled to see that the deer was being chased by a large, hairy, manlike creature running upright on two legs. Both the deer and creature continued into the woods. The driver left the area as quickly as he could.

Chapter 16
More Creature Encounters

Bigfoot Stomping through Pennsylvania
1987
Derry Township

Bigfoot incidents were continually reported during 1987. During this time period residents reported frightful high-pitched screams unlike anything they had ever heard before. Not only were there actual sightings of the creature, but other incidents also seemed to indicate their presence. I also heard accounts of dogs and cats that were frightened, as well as some animals that were missing.

Residents of a mobile-home community were complaining of nighttime prowlers peering in their windows, which were over eight feet off the ground. Some witnesses saw the shadowy figure of a tall creature with brilliant glowing red eyes during the night.

One of the sightings was a creature incident on February 1, 1987, at 2:30 a.m., when the Bigfoot walked out in front of a car in a remote area near Gray Station, where many other incidents have also been reported. The creature walked upright and stood about eight feet tall, with its eyes glowing a bright pinkish-red in the headlights. This witness was able to see two large fangs from the top of the mouth.

In the same general area on April 8, 1987, another witness reported that, as he was sitting in his car, he noticed something dark approaching from the woods, moving in his direction. He turned on his headlights and was shocked to see what he described as a huge, hairy, apelike creature that stood between nine and ten feet tall with eyes that glowed bright red. Its arms hung down past its knees, and it made a loud grunting sound as it approached the car.

He noticed a strong smell of sulfur in the area as the creature approached to within thirty feet of the car, at which point the man spun out of the site in his vehicle, watching the creature in his rearview mirror as he sped way. A short time later he brought another person back to the site, who confirmed the lingering sulfur odor.

Consistently over the years sightings have been in concentrated areas, especially along the Chestnut Ridge area around Latrobe, Ligonier and Derry. This ridge is desolate in many areas, has numerous caves, and has a large population of rattlesnakes. Over the years a number of explores and hikers have reported sightings of these beasts. On the afternoon of May 5, 1987, one such individual in a section of the ridge known as Bear Pond Hollow claimed that he saw such a creature, noting its long stride as it moved through the brush.

Near New Alexandria on May 16, 1987, two men driving down a back road had their passage blocked by a dark, hair-covered, manlike creature that stood ahead of them. As the men approached a bridge, they stopped when they saw the creature. After several minutes of staring at it, one of the men reached for a .22 rifle that was in the car, and fired twice over the creature's head. Finally, it turned and slowly walked away into the wooded area.

Black Panther Seen near Shopping Area
April 20, 1985
North Huntingdon

When two people walked out of a store in the Norwin Shopping Center on Route 30 in North Huntingdon, they sure weren't prepared for what they saw. It was about 7:00 p.m. on April 20, 1985, when the two men looked up to the top of a dirt bank where a construction site sat. At the top of that hillside was a tree line along which they saw a huge black cat. One observer yelled out that it was a black panther. When the animal was first seen, it was walking along the tree line, but then made an abrupt turn and looked down the steep bank. It then swung its long black tail around and walked back into the woods. The animal had a body length estimated to be about three and a half to four feet long, and a three-foot tail. The animal was covered in dense, shiny black hair. The tail was dropped down as it moved, and was thin and curled at the end.

The senior male witness was concerned about seeing a wild animal loose in the area and called the local police, who quickly responded to that location. Two police cars arrived on the scene from two different local police departments, and the man pointed out the location where the animal had been seen. One police unit searched the densely wooded hill on the back side of Barnes Lake Road.

Photo of hillside where black panther was reportedly seen.
Copyright Stan Gordon

While unconfirmed, it is my understanding that the panther came out of the woods again and was reportedly seen by at least one officer as well as the other witness. At another point the head of a large black animal could easily be seen looking out from the brush, and it was reportedly not a dog. The head was seen farther back in the woods from the original sighting location. Some police officers approached that area but found it to be so thickly wooded that they could not enter to search. Once again, the mysterious cat was never found.

I was contacted in regard to this animal observation, and went to the scene of the sighting. I also interviewed some of those involved and found them to be credible.

Two Huge Bigfoot Creatures Seen in Daylight
January 2, 1983
Hempfield Township

It was a winter day in 1983 when two workmen saw something that boggled their minds. It was about 2:30 p.m. on January 2, 1983, in rural Hempfield Township, just a few miles outside of the city of Greensburg. The men were doing some construction work when they noticed two people come out of a house across the road and begin to work on a farm tractor.

About fifteen minutes later one of the construction workers noticed what appeared to be two tall manlike figures walking on a distant hill. As he continued to watch them, he realized that there was something quite unusual about them, and so he pointed them out to his helper. The two creatures began to then walk in a seemingly cautious fashion into a nearby field across the road. The silhouette of their huge bodies could at times be seen against the skyline. The creatures appeared to be black in color, broad shouldered, and with long arms. They seemed to be bent over as they walked.

The one creature suddenly—and seemingly with purpose—moved away from the other creature. Bending down, it picked up something from the ground, then hoisted it over its shoulder. The witnesses were of the opinion that it might have been a deer carcass. It then walked back over to the other creature.

Both creatures then walked into the woods that were about two hundred yards away. The creatures did not appear to be moving quickly, but due to their long legs, their strides let them cover at lot of area quickly. About fifteen minutes later the construction workers watched as the farmers hitched the tractor to a flail and proceeded to move up into the area where the creatures had been a short time before.

They soon realized just how huge the two creatures had actually been. Comparing the size of the men and their equipment with the size of the creatures, they soon realized that the creatures had to be about twelve feet tall and at least twice as broad shouldered as the men. The measurement they used to determine this was that the chute of the flail was nine feet high.

Later the workmen walked over to the site where they had seen the giant, manlike creatures. The ground was partially frozen, but they found some scuff marks on the ground surface in that area. Investigator George Lutz and another man met with the witnesses about a week after the incident at the site. Using two-way radios, they compared the sizes of the men from the location of observation to the spot where the creatures were seen. Doing this, they were able to determine that size of the men was only about half as tall as the creatures, which corroborates their original estimation of height.

When I interviewed the witnesses involved, they were both upset and astonished by what they had seen. Years later one witness related to me how this sighting had an impact on his life.

Bigfoot Active in 1988

Reports of Bigfoot activity increased in Westmoreland and Cambria counties in May 1988 and continued throughout that year. Most of the reports were quite similar, involving a creature walking upright, from seven to eight feet tall, covered with hair, and with long arms. During this time several of the sightings were during daylight hours, and the creatures often were seen at close range. Again, in Westmoreland County, the sightings were concentrated in the Chestnut Ridge area between Derry, Latrobe, and Ligonier.

One event occurred at a farmhouse near the base of the Chestnut Ridge on June 26, 1988. When a family returned home, they found their livestock to be nervous. They became more concerned when they found where a flood light, six feet off the ground, had been cleanly ripped from its socket, along with large footprints around the house. A PASU team arrived at their home a short time later and was able to make a plaster cast of one of the footprints. The print measured sixteen inches long and ten inches wide, although poor ground conditions did not clearly reveal the number of toes.

Three days later the lady of the house was awakened at 7:00 a.m. by a noise. She was startled when she peered out her kitchen window to see a large, hairy creature walking with long strides along the fence line bordering her stables. The color of its hair in the morning sun was described as grayish-brown. Its height was estimated to be seven feet, and it had no apparent neck or waist. Although she took three photographs of the creature, some defect in the camera prevented her pictures from being developed. Previously the family had never had any problems with the camera.

Chapter 17
Pennsylvania's Twilight Zone

The Chestnut Ridge

In 1989, The Philadelphia Inquirer did a feature story on my PASU research group and our investigations. The February 12, 1989, story focused on an area known as the Chestnut Ridge, which has had a long history of strange occurrences that include Bigfoot encounters, UFO sightings, and other assorted oddities.

The ridge, which is part of the Allegheny Mountain system, is about one hundred miles long, and stretches from near Preston County, West Virginia, through Westmoreland, Fayette, and Indiana counties in Pennsylvania. It is thickly wooded, and many caves and hollows make its natural beauty rather shadowy and scary at times. Reporter Carol Morello, after hearing of the many strange accounts in the area, dubbed this "Pennsylvania's Twilight Zone."

Old-timers in the area are familiar with strange events that have reportedly occurred in the ridge area and its surroundings. Since the early 1970s, we have received almost yearly reports from the Chestnut Ridge area. The earliest firsthand Bigfoot encounter that I have on file where I was able to interview the witness in person occurred near Indianhead in Fayette County in 1931.

Among some of the other oddities reported are sightings of panthers, objects crashing into the ridge (originally reported as airplane crashes), mysterious underground sounds, falls from the sky, and geological anomalies. While similar events have been reported in many areas of Pennsylvania and in other states, an unusually high concentration of strange events seem to happen in the Chestnut Ridge area. Whether or not a link exists between the various phenomena has yet to be proven. The question remains as to why such occurrences seem to repeatedly occur in this same mountainous region. The following accounts are examples of some of the events that have taken place in this area.

Strange Activity on a Farm
April 1989
Fayette County

Continuing with strange events in the Chestnut Ridge area, a series of incidents occurred in Fayette County outside of Connellsville. A farmer reported hearing strange screaming sounds of undetermined origin at night. His dogs began to act as if they were frightened of something. It was about dusk during the week of April 16, 1989, when he observed something large walking on his property.

A tall, manlike creature covered with light brown hair walked out of the woods, crossed a road, then went through a field. He watched as the creature easily stepped over the top of a five-foot-high fence, something that was humanly impossibly. He was now sure that what he saw lurking in the area was not human.

It was just days later on April 26—on the same secluded rural property—that another strange event took place. At about 9:15 p.m., the witness observed a cluster of non-blinking red lights move across the sky behind the mountain. Seconds later a brilliant flash of light lit up the horizon in that same part of the sky. He had an initial impression that an aircraft might have crashed, but he did not hear any sound of an impact.

Just minutes later all of the normal background sounds of the woods, such as frog and insect noises, abruptly ceased, creating an eerie effect. Several dogs on the property all became quiet and still. The farmer had never experienced this before.

Fisherman Encounters Bigfoot
April 20, 1989
Donegal

On April 20, 1989, a man went night fishing with his dog at Donegal Lake. The fellow had been there for about ten to fifteen minutes and all was quiet. It was a clear moonlit night when, at about 12:15 a.m., the sound of something rustling in the brush came from behind them. The dog began to bark and then to growl, and the man felt that someone was lurking about the area.

As the fisherman shone his flashlight in the direction of the sound, he caught sight of a seven-foot-tall muscular creature standing upright like a human but with extremely broad shoulders. Its arms hung almost down to its knees, and it was covered with dark brown or black hair or fur. The head of the animal was larger than that of a human, and the eyes glowed a light red color when they were hit with the flashlight beam. The witness estimated that it weighed between three and four hundred pounds. No smell was detected while it was observed.

When the fisherman hit the creature with his flashlight beam, it made three loud shrill sounds or screams in succession, each lasting about a second. These sounds were unlike anything the fellow had ever heard and they truly frightened him. The creature stood still and stared directly at the man and his dog.

Moments later the creature departed into the woods. The witness kept the flashlight beam on the creature as he watched it move off. It took huge strides and walked away on two legs with a slouching posture.

The man and his dog quickly made their way home, where he told his family what he had seen. The encounter was reported to the state police in Greensburg, who patched the witness to my Hotline sighting number. I did an initial interview, and an investigation took place soon after. PASU investigators John Micklow and Joe Kosczuk went to the scene with the witness and scrutinized the area for evidence. The fisherman recalled that he was frightened by what he had seen. In the past he had heard stories of such creatures being sighted, but did not believe those accounts until he had a sighting himself.

Glowing Anomalies near Ligonier
May 20, 1989
Ligonier Township

I received information on May 23, 1989, concerning the following odd event that had taken place in a mountainous area in Ligonier Township. It was early morning, about 1:30 a.m., on May 20 when a man walking his dog observed a brightly glowing "something" resting on the roadway about one hundred yards ahead of him. The glowing object was oblong shaped and light bluish-white in color. He said it looked like a four-foot florescent light bulb, but larger in scale. He estimated its size as approximately eighteen to twenty-four inches wide and three to four feet in length. It was also about as bright as a fluorescent light bulb.

Initially the man thought it was the moon reflecting off of something. After some clouds blocked the moon, he continued to watch and saw that the object never varied in its luminescence, size, or shape. He left the area and returned with two other people, who watched the strange object for about another thirty minutes. While they were all baffled by the object, they were afraid to approach any closer.

Then something else strange occurred. A white picket fence was located about fifty feet from their position. All of the sudden a portion of the fence began to glow "like the luminous dial on a watch at night" and then suddenly stopped after a few seconds. The object remained on the isolated roadway with little traffic in this rustic area. Early the next day they returned to the scene but could find no evidence or explanation for the enigma. They returned again the next night under similar conditions, but nothing further occurred. PASU conducted an investigation into the matter.

Ice Fall near Wilpin
May 21, 1989
Wilpin

Near the town of Wilpin at 8:45 p.m. on May 21, 1989, a man was sitting on his porch when his attention was drawn to some nearby trees. It sounded like something had hit a maple tree, so he walked over to have a look. To his amazement he found that a chunk of ice had apparently fallen from the sky and into the tree. The piece of ice was about the size of the palm of his hand, was mostly flat with a concave area in the middle of the piece, and had a sweet smell about it.

The man contacted his son, who came over and saw the ice chunk as well. The perplexed observers picked up the ice and put it in a plastic storage bag, then stored it in the freezer. PASU members John Micklow and Joe Kosczuk went to the location and conducted an interview. The ice sample was sent to a laboratory for analysis. An analytical evaluation was conducted on the sample by a laboratory that conducted the procedure as a professional courtesy. The following is a breakdown of the results listed in milligrams per liter:

Ice Fall of 5/21/1989

Lead	0.018
Iron	0.32
Cadmium	0.0024
Arsenic	0.001
Aluminum	0.42
Zinc	1.05

The analyst felt that, due to the high concentration of metal in the specimen, it was possible that the ice may have originated from a high-flying aircraft. However, weather data obtained for this area and date indicated a low probability of icing conditions.

Underground Rumblings
March 25, 1987
Derry Township

Once again, unusual events continued to be reported from locations along the Chestnut Ridge. Residents from Derry Township in Westmoreland County were awakened about 3:00 a.m. on the morning of March 25, 1987, by a muffled, rumbling sound apparently from beneath their home. According to a witness, it was like an explosion under the house that lasted only a few seconds, but it shook the house while also flipping a drain cap upside down in their basement.

Another neighbor who lived about one half mile away also reported the same experience regarding the sound and shaking of his home. The Pennsylvania Department of Environmental Resources was contacted, and the witnesses were advised that no underground mining activity was going on in the area that they were aware of. The story was also carried in the March 25, 1987, edition of The Latrobe Bulletin.

A Cattle Mutilation in Fayette County
November 1986

In November 1986, a strange incident occurred on a farm in Fayette County. Speaking with the farmer who owned the property, I learned how he had walked into the field on that day and discovered that his 700-pound Hereford had mysteriously died. The animal was found in a large grassy field where it roamed with the other stock.

When the farmer came across the carcass, he noticed that the end of the tail was cut off down into the bone, yet some of the tail remained attached. The left ear was cut off, along with a section of the head area. The throat was cut into the jugular vein. All of the teats were cut off of its bag. What was most unusual was that there was no sign of blood, not even on the ground. Later it was discovered at the same farm that a bull was also found with the tip of its tail cut off. The farmer noticed in the days just after the attack that his other cattle seemed spooked, and did not eat as they normally would.

Section 3
Diverse Accounts

Chapter 18
More Weird Accounts

Loaves of Ice from the Sky
July 17, 1985
Greensburg, PA

It was a beautiful summer afternoon on July 17, 1985. The temperature was seventy-one degrees, and it was sunny with twenty miles visibility. It was lunchtime for the six maintenance workers at the Westmoreland County Memorial Park cemetery, which is located outside of Greensburg. The men were sitting around when suddenly they caught sight of an object about six feet above the ground falling downward, less than one hundred feet away.

The men all heard a loud thud and then saw fragments shattering and breaking apart in an area about sixty feet wide. They ran over to that location to see what had fallen, and discovered a large chunk of ice. The ice fragment was heavy enough to cause some gouge marks that were several inches deep in the hard ground. The largest fragment of ice was estimated to be about thirty inches in diameter and approximately twenty-four inches thick. The men found numerous other pieces of ice scattered over the grounds, some of which were the size of loaves of bread. The ice itself was clear in appearance, and no smell was associated with the ice.

One of the men gathered up some of the ice samples and put them in a freezer. I was notified of the incident and contacted, then I interviewed the man with the samples the day after the event. Photographs were taken of the area and some of the ice samples were sent to a lab for study.

The most likely explanation was "blue ice." On occasion incidents have occurred where an overhead aircraft has a leak in its toilet facility. The human waste and the added blue chemical used to break down that material can freeze at high altitudes, but usually breaks up or dissipates before reaching the ground. In this case, however, the ice had no coloring; it was clear. The analytical study did not find any bacteria that would seem to indicate blue ice.

Formation in the Field
May 23, 2000
Delmont-Export

It was just a normal day for the couple that lived on a country road between Delmont and Export. At least it was normal until around 3:00 p.m. when one of them looked out their bedroom window toward a tall grass field about forty feet away. There in the field was a large depressed area of corn and tall grass. They had looked out of the window earlier that morning and nothing unusual had been seen.

Photo of the field formation.
Photograph used with permission of the owner.

The family contacted me and I went to that location the same day. The next day I returned to the site with an associate of mine, Jim Mathers, who is a physicist. We measured the affected area and determined that it was about twenty feet by ten feet in size. It was an irregular oval shape.

Jim noted the following details. While examining the site on the second day, we noticed that some of the grass was beginning to spring up again. At one end of the oval pattern, the tall grass was still flat to the ground. The edges of the oval area seemed to be quite sharp.

Photo of the field formation.
Photograph used with permission of the owner.

At one location tall grass strands were standing, while those behind it were knocked down. A definite flow to the direction of the depressed grass could be discerned. In some areas the grass seemed to be layered, where the lower layer seemed to go in one direction while the upper layer appeared at a different angle. That angle may have been as much as twenty degrees.

Some grass samples were obtained, but the samples observed under a zoom optical microscope did not show anything unusual about the affected grass, other than that it had been broken near the ground.

The depressed area could not be seen from the road, and no access by vehicle was available into that field area. What caused this field disturbance has not been determined.

Beams of Light Startle Many
March 2, 1995
Pittsburgh and Other Locations

An unusual light phenomenon was seen in the sky by residents throughout approximately a one-hundred-mile area around Western Pennsylvania. The sightings began about 8:00 p.m. and continued until after 11:00 p.m. They were concentrated in the greater Pittsburgh area, with other similar observations being reported from as far away as Butler and Cambria counties. The observations were similarly described by many people who reported their sighting to my UFO Hotline as well as to various other agencies.

People observed multiple beams of light that appeared to cover the entire sky. A PASU member also observed the phenomenon. The man was traveling through a Pittsburgh suburb when he spotted a beam of light in the sky that he immediately thought was a search light used for commercial advertisements, as these lights are commonly used for grand openings of businesses.

On closer observation he detected beams of light in other locations in the sky. Stopping his vehicle, he noted that there appeared to be fifty to sixty lights extending vertically into the sky in a complete circle of 360 degrees around the horizon. One beam was brighter than the rest, and it looked to be the normal brightness of a search-light beam.

The other lights witnessed were much paler and not readily noticeable. The combined lights gave some observers the impression of a picket fence, but to this observer, they appeared to look like lights shining upward around a circular bowl shape, such as a sports stadium. Using a compass, he determined that the brightest beam, the one he first noticed, was located almost exactly 180 degrees, or at the south magnetic pole.

While observing these lights through binoculars, he saw that the beams did not seem to originate on the ground or from any source that was recognizable in the air. What appeared to be a solid beam under magnification was shown to be made up of many beams together. The beams had no definitive start or end points, but rather ended at the top while the bottom ended in a fuzzy diffused light.

The distinct appearance of these light beams became less distinct, until they faded from view. These lights were visible for nearly two hours. The dimmer beams faded away first, until the brightest, located directly south, was the only one remaining. It finally faded from view at approximately 11:30 p.m.

The Mysterious Fowl Eater
Fall 1982
Pittsburgh Area

In the fall of 1982, George Lutz and I made a trip into a rural location in the Pittsburgh area. There had been recent alleged sightings of cougars, also known as mountain lions, reported from the area. These animals frequented the woods of Pennsylvania many years ago but have been declared officially extinct in this part of the country since the late 1890s.

While we were interviewing a witness who swore that a mountain lion was frequenting the area, we learned of another strange incident that had taken place on a farm at another location.

We had been told that something had apparently broken into a well-constructed turkey pen and had not only killed a large number of the birds, but had also consumed a generous portion of them as well. It was about 3:00 a.m. when the owners of the property heard their dogs bark for just a short time. When the people awakened the next morning, they found two live turkeys on the front porch of their home, which is about seventy feet from the poultry pen. The family members walked down to the pen and were shocked at what they saw.

Nine other turkeys lay dead, scattered about in the snow fence that surrounded the pen. The turkeys each weighed between ten and twelve pounds. The sight was disturbing. Whatever had broken into the pen and attacked the birds had quite an appetite. Each turkey had the breast meat eaten from it, as well as organs such as the heart and liver. Other remains of the turkeys were scattered outside of the pen.

The intruder had entered from the backside of the pen. There were five horizontal boards—each about five to six inches wide and about three-eighths of an inch thick—that had been torn off to gain access to the fowl. The boards were about four feet off the ground, and they were all removed except for the two at the bottom. Whatever had entered the pen had to cross about one foot over a board to get inside. A bar also stretched across the coop where the turkeys would roost.

Whatever had killed the turkeys had apparently taken one out at a time. There was no blood inside the coop. The blood was on the outside and on the ground.

During the night of the turkey attack, the family did not hear any odd sounds or disturbances. The family, though, had noticed in recent months a change in the patterns of a horse and cow staying closer to the house than usual, as if being frightened by something.

During the interview it was revealed that one family member had an experience in early July. This person heard a strange loud sound that was described "like a woman in pain." This high-pitched scream lasted several seconds and scared the person who heard it.

The same night the turkeys were attacked, another report came in of an assault on chickens at a nearby farm. According to reports, several chickens were found totally consumed except for the heads.

It was estimated that between the turkey and chicken kills, a total of about thirty-five pounds of meat appeared to have been consumed that night. It is not known whether one or more creatures was involved or what type of animal wreaked such havoc that night. Could this have been a pack of wild dogs, a mountain lion, or something else even more unusual?

Really Mysterious Pennsylvania

Epilogue

There are many strange mysteries, some of which you have just read in this book, that continue to encroach on our everyday lives. While many such incidents can be explained, many true enigmas continue to occur. Quite often lives of individuals are changed when they experience first hand encounters with visitors from unknown realms. Perhaps you are one of those people. I hope you enjoyed this book and encourage you to report your accounts to me or to one of those listed in the contact information section.

Stan Gordon

About the Author

Stan Gordon was born in Pittsburgh, Pennsylvania, in 1949. Stan was trained as an electronics technician, specializing in radio communications. He has worked in the advanced consumer electronics sales field for over forty years.

Stan's interest in UFOs and other unusual incidents began at age ten. To further his investigations, he founded and directed three volunteer research groups that investigated UFOs, Bigfoot, and other strange occurrences in Pennsylvania for many years. He is a past Pennsylvania State Director of the Mutual UFO Network (MUFON).

Over the years Stan has been involved in the investigation of thousands of strange incidents that have occurred throughout the Keystone State. Referrals concerning these reports have been received from across the state from law enforcement, news media, and other agencies.

Stan is recognized for his extensive investigation into the December 9, 1965, UFO crash incident near Kecksburg, Pennsylvania. He also is known for his firsthand investigation into the major wave of UFO and Bigfoot incidents that occurred from 1973 into 1974. MUFON chose Stan as the recipient of the first MUFON Meritorious Achievement in a UFO Investigation Award for his examination of the September 3, 1987, UFO incident near Greensburg.

Over the years Stan has written numerous articles for various publications on these subjects. He continues to write columns for a national magazine called The Gate. Stan has also been interviewed for scores of local, national, and international newspaper and magazine articles on his investigations.

Additionally Stan's work has been featured on many TV programs and news shows. Some of his appearances include Unsolved Mysteries, Inside Edition, Evening Magazine, A Current Affair, Fox News Channel, SyFy (formerly the Sci-Fi Channel), Discovery Channel, and The History Channel. He has also appeared on numerous radio shows, such as Coast to Coast, Jeff Rense, Night Search, Paracast, Beyond the Edge Radio, and the Mike Pintek Show on KDKA radio.

Stan presents illustrated lectures locally and nationally for conferences, colleges, libraries, and civic and professional organizations, as well as for students of all age groups on topics concerning UFOs, Bigfoot, strange creature encounters, and the Kecksburg UFO incident. Today, as time permits, Stan continues to document and investigate current unusual incidents as an independent researcher.

Contact Information

Stan is interested in receiving reports of UFOs, Bigfoot, and other strange events in Pennsylvania as well as information concerning the 1965 Kecksburg UFO case. He can be reached through the following channels:

Mailing Address

Stan Gordon
PO Box 936
Greensburg, PA 15601

Phone

724-838-7768

E-mail

paufo@comcast.net
sightings@stangordon.info

Website

www.stangordon.info

To order a copy of Stan's award-winning video documentary about the 1965 Kecksburg UFO crash on DVD titled, Kecksburg: The Untold Story, order through his website, or call by phone.

Really Mysterious Pennsylvania

References

Video Documentary, Kecksburg: The Untold Story. Produced by Stan Gordon, 1998.

"Witnesses Sought in UFO Incident." The Daily Courier, Connellsville, PA, 5 September 1986.

Morello, Carol, "Strange Sights Are Common along Chestnut Ridge." The Philadelphia Inquirer, Philadelphia, PA, 12 February 1989.

"Rumbling Noises Reported." The Latrobe Bulletin, Latrobe, PA, 25 March 1987.

Photo/Artwork References:

Kecksburg Pictures: © Stan Gordon

Photo of Pittsburgh: © Stan Gordon

August 26, 1966 incident : Photo of Route 30 Adamsburg: © Stan Gordon

August 30, 1983 incident: Derry UFO, two sketches by Robert McCurry

September 14, 1983 incident: Connellsville, PA (Fayette County), three-toed footprint near pond : © Stan Gordon

December 31, 1984 incident: Level Green sketch of object: Stan Gordon Archives

April 20, 1985 incident: North Huntingdon photo of area: © Stan Gordon

June 21, 1985 incident: Indianhead sketch of UFO by Charles Hanna.

August 31, 1986 incident: New Stanton photo of area: credit George Lutz

December 13, 1986 incident: Gray Station photo: © Stan Gordon

September 3, 1987 incident : Greensburg, PA UFO sketch by Robert McCurry

March 12, 1997 incident: Derry Township photo of scratches on car used with permission of owner

May 23, 2000 incident: Delmont field photos used with permission of owner

September 27, 2002 incident: Derry Township photo of location where creature crossed fence: © Stan Gordon

January 3, 2007 incident: Youngwood UFO photo used with permission of owner

July 10, 2009 incident: Uniontown, sketch of creature used with permission of the Pennsylvania Bigfoot Society (PBS) and Dave Dragosin (artist).

Really Mysterious Pennsylvania

Research Resources
(Web Sites/Contact Info)

Stan Gordon's UFO Anomalies Zone . . . . .www.stangordon.info
To report UFO, bigfoot and other strange incidents:
. . . . sightings@stangordon.info, paufo@comcast.net

BORU—Dan Hageman. . . . . www.boru-ufo.com
Center for UFO Studies. . . . . www.cufos.org
Coalition for Freedom of Information . . . . .www.freedomofinfo.org
CUE—Brian and Terrie Seech
. . . . .www.center-for-unexplained-events.350.com
Inexplicata—Scott Corrales . . . . www.inexplicata.blogspot.com
Jim Brown's Destinations . . . . www.jimsdestinations.com
John Ventre . . . . .www.johnventre.com
Kecksburg VFD . . . . .www.kecksburgvfd.com
MUFON. . . . . www.mufon.com
National UFO Reporting Center . . . . www.nuforc.org
Paranormal Society of PA . . . . www.paranormalpa.net
Patty Wilson . . . . .pineycreekpress@yahoo.com
Pennsylvania MUFON . . . . www.pamufon.com
The Pennsylvania Bigfoot Society . . . . www.pabigfootsociety.com

Breinigsville, PA USA
07 April 2011
259404BV00003B/14/P